About the author

Mavis Jameson Rukin was born in Chorley in 1933 and grew up in Leyland during WWII. For the last fifty years she has lived in Kenilworth in Warwickshire. Having four children over twenty years kept her busy, until she became a mature student at Fircroft College in Birmingham in 1991. There, an argument with another student sowed the seeds for Someday We'll Understand. But it gathered dust when she took full time care of her handicapped grandson after the death of his parents. Many years later, and after much nagging from her family, her first book is complete.

SOMEDAY WE'LL UNDERSTAND

Mavis Jameson Rukin

SOMEDAY WE'LL UNDERSTAND

Vanguard Press

A CIP catalogue record for this title is
available from the British Library.

ISBN 978 1 784653 48 4

*Vanguard Press is an imprint of
Pegasus Elliot MacKenzie Publishers Ltd.*
www.pegasuspublishers.com

First Published in 2018

**Vanguard Press
Sheraton House Castle Park
Cambridge England**

Printed & Bound in Great Britain

Dedication

I dedicate this book to my children Joe and Bonita without whose encouragement this book would never have been finished. My long suffering friend Betty who listened to my stories over tea and cake in our favourite cafe and my late brother Melvin who always brought a smile to my face. Lastly to all you out there who have a story to tell?

You are never too old to dream

Preface

"If you want to know anything about World War II," the lecturer said, *"Ask someone who has lived through it."* And all eyes turned to me. I was annoyed. What did I know about World War II? I was only six when war was declared! I wasn't old enough to have been called up, my town hadn't been blitzed like Coventry or Liverpool, and I hadn't been an evacuee. Besides, I hadn't time to answer the questions that all the other students then bombarded me with. I had come to college to study English, so I could put the flesh on to the bones of a family story. But I made notes of all the questions I was asked, and much to my amazement I began to remember all sorts of things I had forgotten. Old photos and letters from my family brought back memories as did conversations with close relatives. I scoured old newspapers in order to confirm the things I remembered, which to my amazement they did. It turned out my lecturer was right; I was a walking history book, like many of my generation were, though my memory might not be as perfect as it was.

I say 'were' as that was a quarter of a century ago. Unfortunately fate stopped me in my tracks, putting the realisation that I should write a book about what happened on hold. But finally, after so much 'encouragement', or maybe 'nagging' from my children and a friend, and a little nudge from my grandson Alex. I have finally finished what I started at that college many years ago. I hope you enjoy it and perhaps you will find something in the pages that you can relate to or maybe makes you want to find out what you can about your own family story during historical events.

Mavis Jameson Rukin

Chapter One

"Come on, lass, I'm going to take you to see something that you will never forget as long as you live."

It was September 1939 and I was six years old. Prime Minister Neville Chamberlain had made his speech to the nation. The King with a heavy heart had spoken to the people of Britain and the Commonwealth of the sacrifices they would make in the dark days ahead.

Dad put me on the pillion of his motorbike and drove the half mile from our house in Park Street to Chorley bus station where we parked up outside the Grammar School. Opposite on the bus station we saw a mass of frightened, bad tempered people fighting and shouting at each other, with accents and words I'd never heard before, all desperate to get away. Each time a bus came in, a tide of humanity surged forward pushing and jostling each other to get on the bus, the niceties of queuing forgotten.

"Why are they fighting and shouting at each other?" I asked Dad.

"Why! Why?" spluttered Dad. "We are now at war with Germany and them lot," nodding contemptuously over to the chaotic bus station, "are trying to get as far away from here as possible. They know that if German planes ever scored a hit on Euxton this part of Lancashire would go up with one big bang and thousands and thousands of people would die or be maimed." He paused. "All thanks to bloody Kelly."

Puzzled, but certain that was a bad thing as he'd said 'bloody' in front of me, I looked at his angry face and innocently asked, "Who's Kelly?"

He went red in the face and started using more words I'd never heard before, but could only imagine were a lot worse than 'bloody' as he looked up at the sky, looking almost as angry and petrified as the people fighting to get on the buses. So, as curious as I was I thought best not to ask again about Kelly.

Dad was always bitter about what he saw that day. He said most of the people who were fleeing were foreign labourers who had been brought in to work on the construction at Euxton, while at the same time he and his mates had languished on the dole.

Whatever the truth of it, the mass of people I saw fighting each other that day in a desperate panic to get as far away as possible from what they thought would be the German's first target, the literal powder keg that was R.O.F. Euxton, the largest munitions factory in the country, was something that would stay with me forever.

On the first day of the war I had seen first-hand what desperation could do to otherwise decent people. I think that day I grew up a lot, becoming a wiser but sadder child, fearful of the future.

Whilst Dad had gone out of his way to try and show me the realities of war on the very first day, for most people the evidence that there was actually a war on came a fortnight later when petrol was the first thing to be rationed. With all of it being imported and the war at sea starting right away, everyone knew the Navy, Army and RAF needed it. People were issued with dated coupons so they couldn't be hoarded, red for commercial, blue for private use, with red dye put in the commercial fuel to colour the exhaust. Now, anyone caught in a private vehicle with red petrol could face a heavy fine or even jail, which saw the birth of wartime black-marketeering.

But the rationing of petrol was just a small taste of things to come, as on the 29th September 1939 the Government sent out forms to all households in the country, demanding the details of every person living in every home in the United Kingdom. Identity cards, which were just really a bit of cardboard without even a photograph were then issued and everyone was required to carry them at all times. Coded numbers were printed inside the cards which told the authorities each person's status in life.

The ID cards weren't such a big deal really, or at least to me, a six-year-old girl with a Lancastrian accent who was probably not anyone's first guess to be a German spy, it was what came with them: Ration books.

On 30th January 1940 most food was rationed. Everyone was issued with a ration book which they registered at a shop of their choice for each type of produce. There were no supermarkets then, so the meat ration had to be registered with a butcher. Adults had brown ration books, children had blue and pregnant women, new mothers and infants got green, with green books reaping a whole extra two eggs per week and more milk.

They said rationing had to come in to make sure everyone was fed. With less imported food, there would be less food altogether, so prices would go up and people would hoard, and rationing was meant to stop that. We were even told that the banana boats had stopped coming into Preston when the war started, but that meant nothing to our family. None of us had ever seen a banana. There was a girl at school who said she'd once had a banana, but no one believed her. Even if they did really exist, who would be able to afford one?

To put into perspective what rationing really meant, under the Geneva Convention Prisoners of War on British soil had the same rations as the British armed forces.

RATIONS per PERSON

- Meat to the value of 1/2d each week
- 1 shell egg each week
- Butter 2oz weekly
- Cheese 2oz weekly sometimes 4oz
- Margarine 4oz weekly
- Cooking fat 4oz but dropped to 2oz weekly
- Milk three pints weekly sometimes two pints
- Tea 2oz per week
- Sugar 8ozs per week

- Packet of dried egg every three weeks
- Dried milk 8oz every three weeks
- Bacon/ham 4oz every four weeks
- Sweets 12oz every four weeks
- Preserves 1lb every two months
- Offal and sausages were not rationed, at least not yet.

Once a month sixteen extra points were allocated which would allow you to buy 2lb of dried fruit, or 8lb of split peas, a can of fish or a tin of meat, usually Spam. Mam usually got the dried fruit or can of fish. Expectant or nursing (new) mothers, babies and infants got cod liver oil and concentrated orange juice as well as the extra egg and milk. Because of my brother Melvin's age at the start of the war, we picked up cod liver oil and orange juice from the school clinic on Hastings Road. The orange juice was very popular in our house, as were school dinners.

For some reason, 'eating out' was not rationed, and that included school meals, as well as works' canteens. This rule included cafes, restaurants and chippies, though of course you had to be able to afford to eat there. The same was true of pubs, which were the only place anyone could buy alcohol, whether to consume on or off the premises.

There were a few things not rationed, such as the wartime loaf. I became used to it, but it was not popular because of its grey colour; this was because of the recipe that added vitamins and the way it was milled to save energy. But it was good for toasting and what was leftover at the end of the day would be made into Pobs[1] for breakfast. All the grown-ups said that before the nationalised low-energy recipe for bread was introduced, it was not grey; it was something you'd actually want to eat, not simply have to.

Another thing that was not rationed was fresh fish, because the day to day supply couldn't be guaranteed due to the war at sea. This meant the price went through the roof, something one end of our street lamented about every Friday, and with whatever the chippies now had to cook with, fish and chips just wasn't the same. As the war progressed the chip shops opened on a rotary system. The fat smelled awful and you had to be desperate to go to Smokey Joes in Hough Lane.

By the time the Government launched their 'Dig for Victory' campaign, telling people to grow their own food, it was long past when most people realised they had to.

---

[1] Pobs are made from soaking bread in milk and boiling it with a dollop of syrup or honey.

Chapter Two

Whilst Dad taking me to see what the start of the war looked like had made me more than a little scared of what war meant, the mass panicked exodus from Chorley was actually great news for the family as it meant Mam got a job in the powder room at Euxton, weighing gunpowder for shells. Dad, who had become a skilled tripe dresser[2] just as that industry went into a terminal decline, was still on the dole so it meant he would look after me and my little brother Melvin whilst Mam worked.

Mam was a five foot bundle of kindness topped with a head of auburn hair who would help anyone in trouble. During the depression my parents took in a lodger who was down on his luck. When he was due to be means tested by the authorities he asked my mam to say that a valuable grandfather clock was hers should she be asked, the clock was a family heirloom that had been handed down to him for safe keeping. My parents were only too glad to help. They knew if the grandfather clock had been taken by the authorities it would have been sold for a pittance. The authorities did ask Mam if the clock was hers. Shortly afterwards the grateful lodger invited Mam to a very important Gypsy gathering on the Flat Iron in Chorley. When my dad refused to let my mam go the lodger became extremely annoyed. He told Mam that

---

[2] Tripe is the muscle walls from cows' stomachs. 'Tripe Dressers' clean the meat, trim off the fat, then boil and bleach it, ready to be sold.

"She would regret turning down the invitation to the end of her days."

Some months later the lodger moved on, and soon after my parents decided we should move too.

At the start of the war, we lived in a courtyard end terraced house in Chorley; I had to share a room with my little brother Melvin. It was 1940, but the house still had gas mantles[3] and a communal outside lavvy which was emptied each evening by the night soil men. What that meant is there were three outside lavatories (not toilets) which were shared by the eight houses in the courtyard. Unlike toilets, lavvies weren't connected to the sewer system, so were shovelled out each night by men from the council. If that wasn't bad enough, time and time again, you'd find yourself stood outside bursting, waiting in the cold and the rain only to then face the stench the men in the courtyard left behind after a heavy night boozing.

We were now moving to paradise by comparison, to a house that had an outside toilet that flushed just for us and no one else, a front and back garden, a bathroom, and magic lights in every room that came on with the flick of a switch. Best of all, I was going to get a room of my own.

We should have moved in May, but Mam being superstitious[4] decided that we should move to our new house in June, so the first Saturday in June 1940 with my brother clutching our moggy, we all piled into a removal

---

[3] Gas would be fed into a fragile metal mesh. When the gas was lit, the mesh would glow, far brighter than just the flame would have done.

[4] The saying goes: 'Move in May, you're not there to stay'.

van and headed for Leyland, a small industrial town a few miles from Chorley.

Just as we arrived at our new house our moggy, I'm not sure if it ever had an actual name, jumped out of the van leaving a smelly mess all over my brother who then was promptly sick all over the cab. The removal men muttered dark deeds under their breath as they dumped all our belongings unceremoniously on the living room floor. Mam promptly hauled my screeching brother off to christen the bathroom, leaving Dad to sort things out. We never did see our moggy again.

Maybe I should have chased after the cat, but my parents had promised me a bedroom of my own at the new house, so the first thing I did when we arrived at 36 Edgehill Crescent was thunder up the stairs like a baby elephant to lay my claim. The first room I entered was small, it overlooked an extension adjoining the house. This, I later discovered, was our coalhouse. Next to the coalhouse was our very own flushing toilet. I pushed open the door of the second room it was filled with sunshine; the colours of the rainbow danced around the room, reflected from a prism swinging above an open window in the warm afternoon sunshine. This room was going to be mine. I walked into the bedroom to explore further, then moved towards the window which didn't have sash cords you had to pull to open it with, but proper catches. Casting my gaze down into the back garden I saw a swing that had been left by the previous occupants. A room of my own, a real toilet, a garden and now a swing too? Suddenly it seemed like there were some real benefits to being at war.

Beyond the bottom of our garden was a meadow with a number of strange animals I'd never seen before grazing. Even though I didn't know what they were, I could tell from the noise it was making, one of them was in distress. My gaze then turned to watch a rosy faced man as he opened a five barred gate, and ran to the animal, which by this time had a huge balloon protruding from its back. I felt I had probably seen more than I wanted to of this particular scene, and there was still more to explore inside, so I moved on to the third bedroom. This room was darker and colder than the other two; it had a long bay window which took up most of one wall. At each end of the bay were two small windows. I opened the nearest window and looked up and down the street. At one end of the street there was a rickety fence with a stile in the middle, a well-trodden path lead from the stile into a meadow, then following a hawthorn hedge it dipped down towards a brook.

I could see boys swinging from trees on ropes pretending to be Tarzan before falling into the water. Beyond the brook there were fields as far as the eye could see, in fact we seemed to be surrounded by fields. Up the street a crowd of children were playing a skipping game; two children with the end of a rope in each hand turned the ropes alternately while other children ran through the ropes. It looked impossibly complicated to me at that moment in time, but it was going to be one of my favourite games. On the other side of the road a lady was sitting in the front garden enjoying the sunshine; she looked up at me smiled and waved. It was as if she was welcoming me to paradise.

Just then my dad and mam brought the beds upstairs with my grumbling four-year-old brother Melvin trailing behind with the bedding. After making up the beds, which absolutely confirmed I had the room I wanted, we all sat down to have a meal. I was filled with excitement, and couldn't understand why my parents weren't. They were solemnly and intently listening to the weather forecast on the radio, occasionally shushing Melvin and me whenever we tried to talk. The day we had moved house was the day the news of the Dunkirk evacuations, which had been ongoing for a few days, was broadcast to the public. The nation prayed as an armada of little boats from all over the country, many of them tied with ropes behind larger vessels, had set sail to rescue our stranded soldiers on the French beaches. That day was the first time I'd ever seen both my parents cry.

My parents had lived through WWI, when the Germans had been held firm halfway across France for four years. This time, with the Russians on their side, they had taken all of continental Europe that opposed them in just a couple of months. Britain now stood alone, but a couple of days later when Churchill made his 'We shall fight them on the beaches' speech it was if the whole country had fear and despondency turned into a determined resolve, and all the talk that the Government were ready to surrender stopped.

After tea I decided to explore the Crescent. All the houses were semi-detached and had bay windows and identical gated fences with a path leading around the back of the house. A garden across the road caught my eye. I had never seen anything as lovely in my life. In the centre of the garden a path of crazy paving circled a bed of golden marigolds, and in the corners of the garden there were more marigolds interspersed with red flowers; white roses cascaded over the front door creeping into the open windows. The sheer beauty and perfume of this lovely garden took my breath away. The front door opened and a skinny ginger haired man came out followed by an equally skinny ginger headed boy about my age. They introduced themselves as the Dean family, the boy was called Maurice.

"Your garden is lovely," I gushed.

Mr. Dean looked at me for a second. *"You're the new people?"* he nodded to our house.

"Yes we have just moved in," I replied.

"Would you like a closer look at my garden?"

I couldn't wait to get into the garden to smell the roses.

"Would you like to take some home for your mam?"

"Yes please," I said, enthusiastically.

Maurice's dad disappeared into the house. A few minutes later he came out with another boy close behind who was carrying a newspaper and a pair of scissors. This boy was shorter and fatter than the first boy and a little shy.

"That's Dennis; he's my twin," said Maurice

"You don't look alike" I observed, but before I could say anything else his dad handed Maurice two bunches of flowers wrapped in newspaper

"Maurice, carry the flowers over to the little girl's house for her mam," said his dad.

Mam thought the flowers were lovely, but was still wiping the tears away as she put the white roses on the dresser and the marigolds and the red flowers in the kitchen. I thought the red flowers would have looked nicer with the roses, but thought better off not saying anything.

The next day I simply had to explore more of this amazing new world. I found a number of houses in the street were vacant, including the houses on either side of ours. Curiosity took me up the path of the empty adjoining house. As I stood on my tiptoes looking through the front window Maurice joined me. On tracks in the front room we could see a train set that had been abandoned by the previous owner. "When they did a moonlight flit!" said my worldly friend darkly.

Maurice told me he came over most days just to look at the train wishing it was his I also wished it was mine. How could anyone leave a train set behind?

Later that day I asked Dad if we could get the train set 'for my brother'. Obviously I desperately wanted to play with it, but train sets were for boys. He shook his head. "It doesn't belong to us, and besides the people who are moving in next week have a little boy about the same age as Mel."

That evening I heard church bells ringing in the distance. I didn't know it then, but I wouldn't hear them again for five years, when they would be rung out in jubilation to mark the end of the war. For now, church bells would be silenced for the duration, only to be rung again if either the country was being invaded or if peace was declared.

The Bradleys arrived at number 38 before the end of the week; their little boy Derek was delighted with his train set which he and Mel played with most of that summer. The Bradleys had an older son who was in the Navy who I saw briefly when he was home on leave. Shortly after the Bradleys had moved in, number 34 on the other side of us became tenanted with a young married couple. When the husband was called up into the Army his wife became a frequent visitor to our house.

Whilst there was still more exploring to do, the last big part of the move was when my dad took me to my new school, St. John's Infant School, where I would be until I was nine. A few days later I was walking the school with the twins. With only one road to cross it was a pretty safe area as there were few vehicles about at that time.

St Johns Infant School, Earnshaw Bridge, Leyland, Lancashire

Besides the staffroom and the toilets, St. John's was just one big hall. Every morning we would have assembly with songs and prayers, and then the hall was partitioned with a big concertina door pulled down the middle to divide it into two classrooms. The class at the back of the hall was for the younger children, it being nearer the toilets, with the class at the front of the school for the older children. But it wasn't quite that simple, because moving up from one class to the other didn't automatically happen when you got to a certain age; it was also due to ability, meaning some children would never leave the 'younger' class until it was time to go to Junior School. The most certain way of getting moved up was getting to the point where you didn't write with pencil any more, but could manage to dip your steel nib pens in the inkwells in the top of the desk, and write without making a mess.

After the classes had been divided we all followed our teacher into our individual classrooms, and then stood by our desks and waited until we were told to put our gas masks in our desks and sit down, and wait for lessons to begin. The Government had issued everyone with a gas mask, as gas had been used with horrific results in the First World War. Gas masks were just one of the many things made in Leyland, but the ones for younger children like Melvin, with the Mickey Mouse face were horribly creepy, and Melvin thought his was only good for making fart noises with.

Every morning the milk monitors would come around the classroom and place a small bottle, a third of a pint I think, of milk on our desk. In the winter months for a few pence the Headmistress would make us all a nice cup of hot Horlicks. Once when the milk monitor was absent for a fortnight I was given her job. Every evening after school I had to collect the crates of milk from Robinsons Farm across the road, which I then took into the school for the following morning's milk. At the end of the week I was paid sixpence, it was a tiny silver coin of the relm, a very tidy sum in those days, so needless to say I was sorry when the fortnight was up.

In the last week of term that year the Headmistress announced: "If anyone has a brother or sister who will be five-years-old during the summer holidays bring them into school at the beginning of the next term."

I misheard what the Headmistress had said and took my brother into school the same week. Melvin clearly wasn't ready for school yet, as he howled until it was time to go home.

Chapter Three

The summer of 1940 seemed to go on forever, especially with the hot weather. Each evening after tea Dad and I would sit on the back doorstep in the warm sunshine and just talk.

"You know, Mavis, if you sat on a chair at the top of Golden Hill and counted the Chinese marching past you at ten a breast you would be dead before they all had gone past."

I laughed at the thought of sitting on a chair counting hordes of Chinese and turning into a skeleton.

The war brought out the philosopher in Dad, and he often talked of things going in circles and not learning from our mistakes, but that just bored me. Dad wasn't a religious man. He said religion was a means of controlling the masses by the wealthy to protect their interests, but despite this Mel and I had to go to Sunday school at St. John's, where we were given an attendance card with a little proverb on it from the Bible as proof we had been.

Dad didn't talk much about his family, but when he did it was usually about his brother Bill who died in France in WWI. With tears in his eyes he would talk about the last time he saw his brother. Bill had come home unexpected on a short leave, and the first thing he did as he walked through the door was kick the family cat out of the house, explaining to my dad that he had seen cats and rats on the battlefield eating his dead comrades who had fallen in no man's land. Bill told him that it was absolute carnage out there in Europe. The soldiers felt they were being treated as expendable by glory seeking generals and an uncaring Government. The war casualties on the battlefields had decimated the nearby town of Accrington. Whole streets had seen all their sons lost in the trenches. It was so bad the Government suspended recruitment in the town. Dad thought WWI was a way of solving the country's unemployment in one foul swoop. He probably thought the same about this war too.

While his brother Bill slept, Dad washed his socks and the time they spent together talking about the war, influenced Dad for the rest of his life. Dad never saw his brother again; Bill was killed at the age of twenty years on 20th November 1917. He has no grave, but his name was added to the Thiepval Memorial; pier face 50, number 128, along with the rest of his comrades whose bodies were never found on the Somme.

Dad said the survivors of WWI had marched home to dole queues, and soup kitchens, and at the 'Big Lamp' in Chorley the ex-soldiers talked of revolution over their soup and hot chocolate. There had been no big monument built in the market square in Chorley to the fallen soldiers, just a plaque was placed at the top of the stairs in the town hall. In the churches throughout the town, names of the fallen of that parish were remembered on memorial plaques, but Dad said that the families of the fallen had to pay for that privilege.

Dad was never able to pay his respects to his brother, but I promised him that when I grew up I would visit the battlefields and place a poppy by his brother's name.

* * *

I kept the promise I'd given my dad all those years before, when in 2009 at eleven a.m. on the 11th November I stood with my husband at the Menin Gate in Ypres, as thousands of poppies cascaded down in memory of the young men from all over the world who died in that dreadful conflict. It was the first time the Germans had been allowed to march in the ensuing parade. They were respectfully received.

It took over ninety years for Chorley to honour its fallen heroes, but thanks to a few good men that wrong was righted. In February 2010 a monument was unveiled on the 'Flat Iron' in memory of 222 'Chorley Pals' Y Company East Lancashire's who had marched proudly through the streets of Chorley to the railway station on a cold and foggy morning decades ago, never to return.

Theiphval Monument on the Somme

William Jameson was not a member of the 'Y' company so his name is not on the 'Chorley Pals' monument, but on a plaque in the church of St. George in Chorley.

In the autumn of 2014 swathes of red poppies filled the moat surrounding the Tower of London an event known as 'Blood Swept Lands and Seas of Red' where 888,246 ceramic poppies had been planted in memory of all the young men who had died in the 1914-18 war. At eight-thirty p.m. on Tuesday 12th August 2014 William Jameson's name was one of the few whose names were read out at the Tower of London in honour of the many who had lost their lives.

Chapter Four

In the Euxton powder room Mam had been paired up with a lady called Betty Clark who previously had worked in domestic service down south before moving to a little cottage on Fox Lane. Mam and Betty were so well matched they were often mistaken for sisters. Working closely under dangerous conditions day after day brought about a friendship that was to last them all their lives. They both had a keen eye and small hands, so they were perfect for the delicate and dangerous job they had to perform in near darkness.

But like many of the women who worked with cordite, the material that replaced gunpowder, Mam had started turning yellow, with a tinge of orange in her hair and soon enough she had cordite poisoning and had to leave Euxton. She would have to spend time recuperating, but she was going to be all right and at least she hadn't lost all her teeth.

With mam laid up in bed, Dad managed to get a job as a haulage driver for a local garage. This job would take him all round the factories, ports and railway goods yards of the north west, a job that any German spy would literally have killed for.

Soon after, one of the lads from our street who worked with dad was called up for the Army, and he asked my dad to look after his car for him. This wasn't unusual, as it might as well go to someone who knew how to drive, and even in a town that made buses and lorries, there weren't many people who had ever driven. Whilst it was unlikely that Dad would use the car, he did now have two ways to access petrol, either by maybe syphoning it out of his wagon when he was on the road, or by using the ration book that came with the car. We might not want the petrol, but someone would.

When Mam was better she got a job in the canteen at Baxters Rubber Works on Golden Hill, easy walking distance from our home. Getting that job was also great news for the family, as there would always be the chance at the end of a shift that there would be perishable food that had to be eaten that day.

* * *

The war started to become more real that summer as the bombs started to fall. One day at the end of the school holidays, 31st August 1940, two dozen bombs were dropped from Slater Lane to Earnshaw Bridge, but there wasn't one single casualty.

One of the bombs had fallen just yards away from the school, but it failed to explode. This caused a great deal of excitement amongst all the children in the area for it meant school might not reopen for at least a couple of extra days, maybe for longer if it did go off! It wasn't long before Mel and I sneaked off to have a look at the damage. When we got closer to the school we could see Army personnel working on the large metal object in the crater. The bomb seemed massive and was sat in a huge crater just outside the school railings. We were sure that if it went off, it'd take the whole school with it, something that Mel really wanted to happen, and he was already disappointed that there was no shrapnel, something boys treasured. But we were soon chased off by the bomb disposal unit who realised what we didn't, that we were in the potential blast zone.

Much to Mel's disappointment, but my delight, the next day we were told the bomb had been made safe and taken away, so school would reopen after the holidays. A bus shelter now stands where the bomb fell.

On the first day of school in September 1940 Melvin dragged his feet all the way to the school gates, still moaning that *"Those useless Germans couldn't even manage to hit one poxy school."*

At the morning assembly on that first day, the Headmistress blew her whistle long and hard. Then, addressing the entire school she solemnly said, "When you hear me blow three sharp blasts on my whistle, I want you to stop what you are doing, make class lines, and then follow your teacher down into the shelter."

Around that time daylight raids were frequent and the fields around us were always being peppered with bombs by the Luftwaffe as they continued in the search to find MOD Euxton. If we were at school when the sirens sounded the whistle would be blown, we would get our gas masks out of our desks, form class lines and then march in crocodile fashion into an underground shelter adjacent to the school. In the semi darkness we would sit on long benches facing each other and sing 'One man went to mow' and 'Ten green bottles' till our jaws ached. When the all clear was sounded we would emerge into the daylight to find our distraught parents waiting for us in the playground.

Whilst the Luftwaffe searched for Euxton, there were plenty of other prime targets they had no trouble in spotting. Leyland had a sprawling abundance of factories within its boundaries. Three rubber factories spanned the top of Golden Hill, one of which was heavily involved with work for the Spitfire, and also at the top of Golden Hill was Leyland Motors B.X. shop, home of the Covenanter tank, which had just been completed in time for the war.

In the centre of town there were the main Leyland Motors works, with two massive factories straddling the main street of the town called the North and South Works. Eleven thousand worked just at the Motors, but as well as these large factories, the town had numerous small independent factories plus four mills, all working for the war effort, making everything from aeroplane fuel tanks, and camouflage paint, to parachutes. A great prize indeed for the Luftwaffe.

The raids were starting to get more common, when on 21st October 1940 the Luftwaffe made a direct hit on Leyland Motors Foundry at the top of Golden Hill. The explosion badly damaged the foundry and blew the foundry roof off as well as a door, trapping one poor man underneath as everyone else ran out and headed for the nearest pub on Chapel Brow.

However, the furnace had been left on full burn, so it needed attention. The manager went down to the 'Queens' to get the men back to work to finish their shift, but unfortunately he had difficulties. As one man explained, "We were too pissed up to go back to work."

Besides the foundry, there were also hits on the Axle and Tank Engine Factories before the plane flew on, strafing the glass roof of a textile mill nearby, with the flying glass inflicting injuries on fleeing workers and causing a great deal of damage. The mill had to close for repairs, with some of the workers redeployed to the munitions factory at Euxton.

* * *

There were no fairies at the bottom of our garden, just an Army dugout with a big gun that appeared in the night like a silent mushroom. One chilly morning I drew back my bedroom curtains but instead of seeing cows gathered at the bottom of Broadfield waiting to be taken up to the shippon for milking, I saw the comings and goings of Army personnel in the meadow. During the early hours of the morning whilst everyone was sleeping a camouflaged netted dugout had been built with sandbags.

For the first few weeks the Army dugout was a novelty for all the other children from the streets. They would hang over the five barred gate at the bottom of Broadfield Drive just gawping at the soldiers and generally making a nuisance of themselves. Sometimes they would shout at the soldiers, but after a while they got bored and drifted away. After the children it was the turn of their mams who would climb over their garden fences with pots of tea and freshly baked cakes, using any excuse to find out what was going on, but they soon got short shrift from the soldiers. It wasn't long before things got back to normal and the Army dugout with its ack-ack gun became just a normal part of our neighbourhood. Barrage balloons that were meant to be a hazard that kept German planes higher in the air went up in the distance, but they didn't last. I don't know why, but they had been getting loose and floating away. Maybe they proved to be just as much of a hazard for our own pilots, or maybe they were sent to nearby Liverpool or Manchester, which would end up getting regular poundings from the Luftwaffe.

That was until one Sunday afternoon, 27th October 1940. I was at the bottom of the street with some friends playing the skipping game 'bumps', which I had seen when I first arrived on the Crescent. What had seemed so complicated then was second nature now. But we all stopped skipping when we heard the drone of a lone plane, getting louder and louder as it came towards us. We were used to seeing planes going overhead and would play guessing games as to what kind they were. But this plane was different. As the droning continued to get louder and louder as it got nearer and nearer, we realised we had never heard an engine that hummed like that. It just wasn't right, and it was so low it seemed like it was about to crash. Before anyone could win our guessing game and shout "German!" the front doors in the Crescent all seemed to open in unison as hysterical parents ran out, screaming and dragging their protesting offspring to safety. Mel and me, as well as a couple of neighbours' children, all ended up under our kitchen table there we stayed until we heard the all clear, more than a bit aggrieved, because we'd missed the action.

The Crescent was filled with gossip; the plane had come from the direction of Southport, but how had it got so far inland without coming under fire? And what about the ack-ack gun in the meadow behind our house, why hadn't it fired at the plane? The pilot was so low he could have sprayed us all with machine gun fire, but for some reason he didn't.

Some of the neighbours reckoned they could see the pilot: "Wasn't he that Leyland Motors premium[5] who used to lodge in Tupp Row before the war?"

---

[5] A 'premium' was a fast-tracked apprentice. Parents or a sponsor would pay for the premium to work for a short while in many areas of the business, with an eye to going straight into management.

"What about the German who lived at the top of Golden Hill?"

"No it can't be him; he is on the Isle of Man for the duration."

Rumours of spies and espionage spread through the streets like wildfire. When we heard that the plane had been shot down and crashed in the Midlands we all cheered, but our cheers turned to dismay when we heard the plane had jettisoned its bombs three miles away over Lostock Hall, killing a large number of people, including a family of eight sitting down for their Sunday lunch. I once visited St. Andrew's Church in Leyland to pay my respects to the Watkins family who lost their lives that sunny Sunday afternoon.

When Dad heard the news, all he did was mutter, "Bloody Kelly"

"Who's Kelly?" I asked for the second time, and once again I was met with was a glare and a stony silence.

Many people were sure at the time why there was a lone low-flying German bomber in the area in daylight; that it had come on its own to avoid detection, and it had come here in daylight to find Euxton. The Germans knew it was around here somewhere, and if they did find it, they would only need the one bomb to set our part of Lancashire alight with a terrible loss of lives. But it was worse than that, whilst the neighbours who said they recognised the pilot had been dismissed by some, it turned out they were right. The pilot had indeed worked at Leyland Motors, installing machinery at the B.X. and he had lived at Lostock Hall, where his bombs had landed.

This news could not have gone down well with the adults. With one of the migrant workers who helped build the B.X. being sent back by the Germans to bomb it, they might not have been saying it, but they were surely all thinking about where all those migrant workers who helped build Euxton were now.

Later that week, on the 30th, the axle factory was bombed again, but thankfully this this time, the bombs failed to detonate. But one time, an incendiary that had come down on the foundry had been perfectly dropped by the Germans with absolute precision. It landed in a pile of sand in the casting shop, exactly where it needed to be to put itself out!

Chapter Five

It was these incidents that convinced Mel and me that we should build our own air raid shelter in the back garden. Communal shelters were being built in the streets all over the town by the Government. One such shelter in Mead Avenue on the other side of town had become a den for the local lads to smoke and play cards in. That was until the local bobby caught them and 'confiscated' their gambling pot, which seemed very unfair, because smoking and playing cards was exactly what the ARP wardens used the shelters for. Mam thought building our own shelter was a great idea, as she had always said that communal shelters usually stank.

The task of building our own shelter would also keep my brother away from playing war games over by the brook with the older boys, at least for a while. Whenever Mel played in the field with the bigger boys, more often than not they would start brook jumping, which was exactly as it sounds, taking a running jump towards the brook, and trying to leap over it. The older boys, with their longer legs would easily make the distance, whilst Mel wouldn't. Landing in the brook wasn't as simple as getting his feet wet, as wartime utility boots were partly made from compressed cardboard, so if he got them too wet, they would fall to pieces, and hewould get walloped by Dad, and Mam would have to use the family's precious clothing coupons replacing them.

So one sunny morning during the school holidays we began to dig out our shelter. The soil was sandy so we made quick progress. Mam kept popping out with jugs of homemade lemonade and cake, and soon it wasn't long before we had dug a deep wide hole. All it wanted now was a big sheet of corrugated steel to finish the job and 'hey presto' we had our own shelter. It would be a surprise for Dad when he came home.

And a surprise it was!

Dad came home from work in the early hours of the morning in the blackout and fell right into the hole Mel and me had spent all day digging, gashing his leg rather badly. He was none too pleased to say the least, but when Mam told him we made the shelter to keep us all safe we didn't get walloped.

When I helped Mam to dress his leg I was shocked to see how little flesh he had on his legs, both of them seemed to be just a mass of blue veins. Mam said it was due to a scalding accident he'd had when he was a child and that was why he was not called up for active service – he was a grade four, but depending how long the war carried on for, he might still be called up.

Soon after Dad fell into the hole, and much to Mel's delight, Dad said he thought we should have a dog to keep us company when he was working away. True to his word one Friday night he came home with a little furry black and white bundle under his coat which Mel promptly christened Bonzo. It was love at first sight for the pair of them. Now, whenever Mel took Bonzo over the fields, it wasn't Mel who tumbled into the house soaking wet but Bonzo. There might have been more of a mess, but at least Bonzo didn't need new boots! When Mam caught the pair of them snuggled up in my brother's bed for the second or third time it was decided that Bonzo should have a kennel. One Saturday Dad arrived home with a considerable amount of wood and built Bonzo a very large kennel. It was just as well, because whenever Mel went missing or it was raining that's where you'd find the pair of them tucked up as snug as bugs in a rug.

Every Friday when I got off the school bus it was my job to pick up six cakes and six barm cakes (which were much nicer than the 'wartime loaf', but more expensive as a result) up from the corner confectionary shop at Earnshaw Bridge for Dad's bagging[6]. One particular Friday I had to stay late at school so it became my brother's job to pick up the cakes. When I got off the bus I found him waiting for me. I asked him had he picked up the cakes. *"Oh yes"* he said, quite proud of himself.

"Where are they?" I asked.

"I put them in the kennel, Bonzo is guarding them."

When Dad asked about his cakes, Mam said they had been sold on.

---

[6] Bagging: Lancastrian for 'packed lunch'.

Chapter Six

There was one thing that we wanted for during the war, and that was a good fire.

Every morning Mam would twist rolls of paper, put them in the fire grate, then after carefully placing the coal in between the twisted paper she would then light the paper and in no time at all we had a fire big enough to warm the cockles of our hearts. But when Dad was at home he would make the fire.

"You seem to be using a lot of coal these days," he said, addressing Mam.

"I don't think so," replied Mam.

Dad frowned. "It's just that the coalhouse seems a bit bare these days, are you sure you aren't being short changed with the deliveries?"

"No, Dad," chirped my brother. "Me and Mavis always count the bags of coal."

I had to agree with Dad, the coalhouse had of late looked a bit depleted.

"Well then if we aren't using more coal, and the coalman isn't short changing us it's being pinched."

At that we all piled out into the back garden to take stock of the coal. When the coalhouse door was fully opened we all had to agree that our coal wouldn't last us to the next delivery, which wouldn't just mean the house was cold, it would mean we couldn't cook food.

Just then the back door to number 38 opened and Mrs B joined us. "I think my coal has been going as well," she said, nodding to her coal house.

On hearing the commotion Maggie from number 40 hopped over the garden fences to join us. "You've got a broken panel at the bottom of the door," she pointed out.

"You couldn't get much coal through that," said Dad, scornfully.

"You could if you had a small hand like mine," said my brother.

"It would have to be at the end of a long arm," I muttered sarcastically.

"Oh no," said Maggie. "You could get quite a lot of coal out of the shed if you knew how."

Without further ado she hopped back over the fences and disappeared.

"You know she keeps her coal in the bath," said Mrs. B nodding at the departing figure.

But before anything else could be added, Maggie came back with a cow rake which she poked into our locked coalhouse drawing out quite a substantial amount of coal. My parents and Mrs. B were speechless, too stunned to say a word.

Not only did Dad mend the broken panel that night, but he fortified the back of the door with a piece of steel he had managed to acquire from somewhere, and Mrs. B changed the lock on her coal shed the very next day. We had no problems with missing coal after that.

* * *

Maggie was a familiar figure in the Crescent who was 'once seen never forgotten'. Most mornings I would see her slovenly, wiry figure scurrying past our window up to her widowed mam's house in the more affluent part of the Crescent. Fag in her mouth, smoke trailing behind like the wake of a ship, never a coat on come rain or shine. Some said she was a rough diamond, others said she was a harridan to be treated with caution. Later when her children came along they would straggle behind their mam, happily sucking on empty bottles on their way up to Grandma's house.

"Do you know?" she said addressing me one day, "they drink a whole bottle of milk a day."

If anyone critised her merits as a mother she would defend her children with the ferocity of a tiger, as more than one luckless neighbour had found out. Given how filthy she always was, it was hard for me to believe that prior to us moving into the Crescent, Maggie had had a big top and tails white wedding that was talked about in the street for years, and even by today's standards most of us would envy. Maggie wasn't afraid of work. Every October she would answer the Government's call for the public to work alongside the Land Army, potato picking at one of the farms on Longmeanygate at Earnshaw Bridge, a truly back breaking job to do all day without machinery. Maggie was a colourful character in the Crescent even though the colour was usually mahogany.

Leyland Motors soon began recruiting female labour for shift work, with Mrs. B getting a job in the nozzle shop in the North Works. Because of the shortage of manpower, women were employed on shift work to work as welders alongside men, which did cause problems with toilet arrangements, as no one had ever thought until now that the factories would ever need women's toilets.

Unlike many other parts of the country, women weren't brought into the factories because all the men had gone off to war, but to increase production. Whilst many of the men had volunteered or been called up, many who had tried to enlist had been turned down. The experience of Frank, who had tried to sign up at the start of the war and many years later would become my brother-in-law, was typical of many.

"So, Mr. Rukin, are you currently in work?" asked the recruiting officer in a tone that suggested he'd asked that question hundreds of times already.

"Oh yes, sir, I work at the B.X., The Motors Tank Works."

"And is it a skilled task that you perform?"

"Oh certainly, I'm time served, been at the Motors since I left school."

"Well then, I suggest you get back to the Motors and make some more tanks. You'll be a lot more bloody use to the war effort there than you will be getting shot at in some muddy field in France."

When Mrs. B started work at the factory, she tried to convince Mam to apply for a job at the nozzle hop, to make it easier to juggle the babysitting between them, but Mam was happy in the Rubber Work's canteen. The job didn't pay as much as the Nozzle shop, but the hours suited her better.

After Mrs. B started work in the nozzle shop I didn't see her again without a turban on her head. It didn't matter if it was work or home, or even getting dressed up to go out, she always wore a turban, and with her large body and small head I thought she looked like a piece of jigsaw. Factory management encouraged the women to wear turbans in order to protect their hair from getting fast in the machinery, and they also helped to prevent static electricity. Most women disliked this cumbersome headgear, until they realised it did have other uses. Smokers used their turbans to hide their cigarettes and matches, and they were also used to take contraband out of the factories or 'foreigners' as they were called. Yes, even in wartime, people nicked stuff from work. I remember Mrs. B. brought home steel ball bearings for us to play with. One steelie was worth three marbles, but the only trouble with steelies was they could smash the glass marbles if you hit them too hard.

Bread knives, extending toasting forks, pokers and flat iron stands all came out of the factories. The favourite item was the brass cat ashtrays which were made in the Motors foundry. The ashtrays were highly prized and bartered for other goods, though why they were still making these at the same time as ornate railings were being torn down to be recycled, I don't know.

There are still some of these 'foreigners' around today, probably on the mantle above your great grandma's fireplace.

Chapter Seven

Before the war when we lived in Chorley, it was the custom to visit my maternal grandparents every Sunday for a family gathering, to what my mam's youngest sister Mildred called 'high tea'. The high tea consisted of toasted barm cakes slathered with butter, followed by a delicious Victoria sponge cake. I always looked forward to high tea, as I got to play with cousin May, who was just a week younger than me, and when we had eaten our fill May and I would run up the stairs to a little box room which contained a big theatrical chest full of beautiful clothes. There we would spend the next hour happily playing dressing up.

Once I found a large glass marble in the chest. I was just going to shoot it across the floor when Grandma appeared. She was very angry; the glass marble I was playing with was her crystal ball which she used for fortune telling. Grandma must have been a good fortune teller because according to mam, wealthy clients used to turn up on the doorstep in Rolls Royce's and whisk her off for a few days. Her son's Phillip and Bobby were delighted when this happened as it meant they would get ice cream when she got back. But one day much to their disappointment their mam arrived home with a crystal chandelier in payment for her services, the chandelier was quite out of place in a working class household; however, the family doctor took a shine to the chandelier and when sometime later grandma had difficulty in finding the money for the doctor's services he took the chandelier in payment. Grandma was not a hand's on lovey dovey kind of person, but she was the one called on to help bereaved neighbours wash and lay out their loved ones, and often helped with their confinements. It seemed that every time the family met up, downstairs in the kitchen my Aunt Irene would be practicing a new dance routine, whilst Aunt Mildred had the job of looking after her young nieces and nephews. The adults would be in the living room in deep conversation about events in Europe, then after putting the world to rights they would reminisce about days gone by.

One story that always cropped up was when Grandad and Mam's eldest brother Danny cycled from Yorkshire to Lancashire looking for work. Grandma, who had been pregnant at the time, had gone on ahead, walking, with my mam and Aunt Marshall to look for a house. They had moved to Yorkshire to find Grandad work in the coal mines, but when that dried up they decided to move back, and Grandma didn't want her child born in Yorkshire. After walking for miles they found a cottage in Westhaughton. Grandad and Uncle Daniel quickly followed and got work at Chequerbent working for the Hulton Colliery Company. A few years earlier in 1910, there had been a mining disaster which had taken the lives of 344 men and boys two days before Christmas Eve, so according to Grandma it was an unlucky company to work for, and the name Hulton was synonymous with the Peterloo Massacre in Manchester nearly a century earlier. Despite all her misgivings they stayed in Westhaughton for a few years before Grandad got a job at the mine in Coppull and moved back to Chorley. They got a modern council house, which not only had a large garden, but most important a bathroom and even an *inside* toilet!

I liked going to my grandma's house it always smelled of lavender. Silver cups shone from all corners of the room, with pride of place given to a gleaming silver shield on a highly polished dresser. All these treasures had been won at various events in Lancashire by Grandad's Morris dancing troupe 'Spick and Span'. When Grandad wasn't working down the mine he was working out dance routines for his troupe of dancers. The troupe performed all over Lancashire winning many cups. They performed at the 'All England' finals at Belle Vue in 1930 – at the Crowning of the Railway Queen – winning the first prize with a routine danced to the tune of 'The Old Rugged Cross'.

Granddad Goodman and his troupe of Morris Dancers, 'Spick and Span'.

Many years later whilst talking to one ex-dancer she told me a little about her time with the troupe: "We were the best troupe in Lancashire; other troupes were always upset when they saw that 'Spick and Span,' had turned up at their carnival. We always had a brass band behind us, because we always danced for the people who lined the streets. Our uniform was a red, white and blue costume with white pumps that had bells on the end of our laces. Our first set of clothes we had was made from white material that had been dyed red and blue, but the second time we wore that uniform, it rained heavy and all the colour ran down our arms and legs. Mrs. Goodman had a dress made of the same material, not only did the dye come out, but her dress shrank."

"How did you get to the carnivals?" I queried.

"We travelled in a wagon with tarpaulin sides. During the week it was used for haulage, but when we were going to a carnival on a Saturday the owner, Mr. Poxon, cleaned it and put bus seats in for us. Friday night was our practice night. Mr. Goodman would put us through our paces ready for the judges, if we didn't get it right he'd bang his sticks together and say, "I'm not taking anybody away tomorrow if you can't do it properly." He was a perfectionist, he wanted the best out of everybody, and he got it. He was a wonderful person, a hard worker, and a very talented man. There wasn't much he couldn't do. They used to call him 'The Man with the Magic Sticks'. Once before a carnival, his sticks were stolen by a rival troupe in the belief we would lose."

"And did you?" I asked.

"Heavens no, the magic was in the man, not his sticks."

"Did you ever lose?"

"Oh yes, but we always came away with a prize. We won the shield outright at Skelmersdale because we had won the cup three years on the trot. We always used to sing 'Oh Mary we crown thee with blossoms today'. If we didn't sing that we didn't win first prize. When we won the 'All England Finals' at Belle Vue we won it with the cross routine. A jazz band played the opening bars to 'The Old Rugged Cross' then little Bobby cracked his sticks; we formed groups of four and danced to the music in the formation of a cross. When it came to the words 'exchange it one day for a crown' we came out of the cross and danced into a beautiful red, white and blue crown, then we crowned our mascot. The people clapped and cheered; we knew then we had won.

"As well as being presented with the cup the whole troupe were given individual medals. One of our group was a young handicapped lad who was so proud of his medal, that when he died he was buried with it. After winning at Belle Vue we were all invited over to Lord and Lady Jackson's home at Withnell for afternoon tea and photos. We weren't just a troupe of Morris dancers we danced on the stage as well. Mrs. Heywood, Mrs. Frances and their marvellous band of sewers made our costumes for when we went on the stage and when we were together as 'Spick and Span'. We had regular social nights to raise funds; we even got permission to take round collection boxes when we danced in the streets. They were the happiest days of my life."

This sentiment was echoed by other ex-dancers I met in later years.

* * *

In February 1939, tragedy struck. My mam's beloved sister Marshall died in childbirth. I never did understand

51

why she had been called 'Marshall' and always thought that a deaf old vicar who didn't notice she was a girl must have christened her that after hearing 'Michelle' or 'Marsha' wrong. Grandma looked after the baby boy who was called John until he was adopted by the nurse who delivered him and renamed Malcolm. Marshall's husband, Uncle John, was a builder by trade and I'm not sure if he tried looking after my three cousins; Marlene, Ronald and May to start off with, and although Uncle John would easily have been exempt from active service in the coming war on compassionate grounds, he joined up taking his grief with him, and spent the rest of the war in Burma. My cousins went to live with their paternal grandparents and I didn't see them again for thirteen years.

My grandma never forgave my uncle for the death of her daughter, as they had been warned when Marlene had been born that she would die if she had another child.

* * *

Later that year the rest of the family gathered for high tea for the last time. It was a muted affair. Aunt Irene was ironing, Mildred was nowhere to be seen and without my cousin May to play with I was bored. I walked into the back garden then wandered around to the front of the house on the other side of the road. I saw a white haired rosy faced man bending down over some brightly coloured flowers. I knew from my parents' description that this was my paternal grandfather, Grandad Jameson, or as my grandparents called him 'a queer old stick'. There had been some sort of falling out with him and Dad, so even though he lived on the same street as my other grandparents, this was the only time I remember ever seeing him.

After watching him for a few minutes I wandered over. "Hello, what are you doing?" I asked.

The old man slowly creaked up he looked me up and down for a second then replied, "Tying up the chrysanthemums."

"They are beautiful. Do they smell?" I queried.

"They do have a smell but it's not a rosy smell." Then changing the subject he asked, "Would you like to see my back garden?"

I nodded eagerly then followed him around the side of the house into a lovely garden full of bright colours and perfumes. He must be rich I thought, because he grew flowers and not vegetables like my other grandad did across the road. I looked at the garden and sighed. One day I will have a garden like this. Minutes later I walked back across the road with my arms full of his precious flowers. I didn't think he was a 'queer old stick' as he looked just like Father Christmas, and in giving me all those flowers he'd acted like him too.

Chapter Eight

The war had now brought prosperity to our family and my parents could now afford a babysitter to look after my brother and I until Mam came home from work. Although food and clothes were rationed, we got a fair share. The rations that we didn't like such as cheese, Mam bartered for something that we did like such as jam. She rationed at a grocer in the town and with a mobile butcher who came into the Crescent once a week. When the butcher began having problems with petrol rationing, Dad managed to 'find' him the odd gallon of petrol, which in turn saw the butcher slipping Mam a few sausages and bits of offal. I once heard him say to Mam, "Without the petrol I get from John I couldn't do my deliveries."

Our milk was delivered by two elderly ladies who did the rounds of the streets each morning with a milk churn, knocking on doors and pouring it out into householder's jugs, but later on, probably because the Government wanted to make sure a pint of milk was actually the same pint of milk for everybody, it was delivered to the doorstep in bottles with cardboard lids. We bought our bread from Sumner's farm at the top of Broadfield Drive, and once a week the ladies from the farm drove a horse and cart into the street to sell fruit and vegetables. In the early years of the war, a rag and bone man would rattle down the street calling for rags, pans, smoothing irons or any bits of metal that we could donate for the war effort; in return he would give out plates or cups.

One commodity we were always short of was soap. Mam got one small packet of Persil and a block of Fairy soap each week, but by the end of the week all we had left was a sliver of soap. We would squash this together with all the other slivers we had collected from previous weeks and added it to a soap ball. The soap ball was used every time we had a bath – in the recommended six inches of water. Fortunately we lived in a soft water area so we could use the globby ball of soap remnants for our hair. The softer toilet soap which you were meant to wash your face with was a luxury we couldn't afford, and shampoo was unheard of in our house. When my mam's younger sister Aunt Irene stayed with us for a couple of days she would always leave us the residue of anything she had left when she went home. Whenever we paid a visit to our grandma and grandad Goodman we would always take a pint of milk, a little bit of tea and our cheese ration, Grandad being partial to a bit of cheese. Grandad had a large garden at the back of his house which always seemed to be filled with rows of potatoes, vegetables and fruit so we always came back home with something out of his garden.

Dad's work as a wagon driver took him to Ministry of Defence factories all over the North West, which was no easy task since all the road signs had been removed for the duration of the war. Security was tight at the M.O.D factories. Not only did Dad have to carry his identity card he also had to have a special I.D. card which was checked each time he drove through the factory gates. After his wagon had been loaded up with wooden crates he would take them over to Liverpool Docks; when he arrived at the docks the dockers would unload his wagon for him, then when his wagon was empty he would drive back to pick up another load. One day he had just delivered his load when the docks came under attack from enemy aircraft. Dad took shelter under his wagon. The dockers began waving their arms and shouting at him to get from under, but he stayed put. When the all clear was sounded he asked the dockers why they were shouting at him. What he believed to be engine parts for the ships was ammunition. Had the German plane scored a hit on his wagon half the docks would have gone up, him included.

One day Dad 'acquired' a gallon of white petrol to go in his loaned little Austin car and announced that he was taking us for a picnic in the countryside. Excitedly, Mel and I helped to fill a bag with paste sandwiches and bottles of lemonade and dandelion and burdock, and taking along Maggie's sister Mary-Anne we all squashed into our little Austin to go for a ride in the country for a picnic. When we had gone just a few miles, a combination of the condition of the road and the rickety suspension shook up one of the pop bottles enough for it to burst all over us, frightening the life out of us all and spraying us all with dandelion and burdock, which Melvin tried to lick off the windows before Mam could wipe it all up.

After that excitement I quickly got bored. I wound the car widow down to get a better view of the countryside, but instead I saw the shells of rows of bombed out houses of Liverpool, and then the most awful smell filled the car making us all cough. "What's that smell?" I asked Dad.

"Dead horses. Shut the window," snapped Dad.

I knew it wasn't dead horses because the grownups had started crying. Dad turned the car around and we drove home in silence. The awful smell that wafted over the city and into our car was from dead people still buried under the rubble.

Looking back Dad should not have taken us, we should not have gone; we were only intruding on people's grief. The only excuse I have is that we were children looking forward to a ride in a car. If the beaches around Liverpool and Southport had not been out of bounds or covered with barbed wire, we probably would have gone there.

Liverpool, like Coventry, had suffered great civilian loss. Dad couldn't explain to us the terrible suffering of the city, but like the way he had taken me to the bus station at the start of the war, he clearly had wanted to show us the realities of the war, and maybe how lucky we were.

Dad told us that there were times he couldn't get through to the docks because of the previous night's raid, but with help from the Liverpudlians they dug his way through. He would tell us about the cockroaches streaming out of the bombed houses, with cries of *"Get the queen! Get the queen!"* Amid all that devastation the Liverpudlians chased a grey dusty white cockroach in a frenzied burst of fruitless activity. Not only were the cockroaches fast, but they were all covered with grey dust. It was into one of these streets that one day Winston Churchill's cavalcade arrived; Dad said the Prime Minister was waving in an empty street much to the amusement of the curious onlookers who had stopped work to view the spectacle. Later that week Winston Churchill's visit to Liverpool was shown in cinemas up and down the country, with him waving to cheering crowds. The reality was that the enemy bombing had caused a bread shortage and riots had sprung up in various parts of the City, so the visit by the Prime Minister was seen by many as a propaganda exercise to lift up the spirits of the Liverpudlians and the rest of a besieged country. One of the happier stories that dad told me was about the Mersey Ferry 'Royal Daffodil 11' after making several trips to rescue stranded soldiers from the beaches of Dunkirk the ship was holed below the water line by enemy planes. The Captain ordered everyone over to the other side of the ship, this lifted the hole above the water line and the ship managed to limp home all because of a brave Captain and crew with nerves of steel.

One Sunday afternoon the lads from the top of the street challenged the lads at the bottom of the street to a football match. A ball was produced and coats were placed by the rickety fence at the bottom of the street and in front of our house to mark the goalposts. The match started off lively and good humouredly with supporters from each side noisily egging their team on. The door of number 42 opened and the newly arrived extended family from Liverpool came out to join in the fun. The head of the house was wheeled out of the house by his wife accompanied by two children and an ancient grandmother. The lads from the bottom of the street scored the first goal which was quickly followed by another. When they scored a third goal in the second half, things got really heated. Insults of 'Proddy Dogs and Red Necks' were traded by both sets of supporters. The situation got out of hand when the losing team turned on the newly arrived family from Liverpool. Distressed they fled indoors. It was at this point the referee called off the match in disgust. The family had not only been bombed out of their houses, but the father had lost his legs in defence of his country.

Shortly after, the family returned to Liverpool; they would rather face the Luftwaffe than spend another day in Edgehill. It was not a proud day for the street.

Chapter Nine

With only the radio to while away the long winter nights we made our own entertainment. If Mam wasn't too tired she would play snakes and ladders with us or draughts. Occasionally I would get down on the floor to play marbles with my brother Melvin, but most of the dark nights were spent helping Mam to make peg rugs. We didn't give our old clothes or coats to the rag and bone man any more; instead we spent the winter nights cutting them up into six inch strips which Mam would then thread into the back of a clean flour sack. No material was wasted, nothing was ever thrown away. When the first rug was finished it would take pride of place in front of the fire. Any others we made would be placed in the bedrooms, but of course there was usually a squabble as to who had the next rug.

Our house, unlike most of the houses in the Crescent had linoleum on the floors upstairs as well as downstairs. All the rugs we made helped to take away the cold bareness of the house, as well as adding a bit of colour and warmth, especially upstairs when Jack Frost had been about during the night painting beautiful intricate ice pictures on the windows inside and out. Occasionally we would wind darning wool around cardboard milk bottle tops. When we had done enough we would stitch them together to make netted shopping bags. We didn't have to give any coupons for the darning wool because it was sold in twelve inch strips. The only colours available were black and brown; however with a little imagination a colourful appliqué would make all the difference to the finished bags. There was no end to our ingenuity.

In the early part of the war when Dad was at home at weekends, we would all gather around the fire, Dad would take out his harmonica, then after playing a few marches he would accompany us while we all had a good singsong. Mam was a good singer her favourite song was 'Violetta' which she sang and I harmonised to. Dad had been a member of a harmonica band in Chorley so he was quite an accomplished player. The band performed in local cinemas during the interval before the main feature. Dad said the band was quite popular with the audiences, who would sing along to the music then give a rousing cheer when the band had finished.

Around seven thirty Dad would put his harmonica away and Mam would go into the kitchen and place two house bricks in the kitchen oven. When the bricks were hot she would take them out wrap them up in a cloth then place them in our beds. Shortly after my brother and I would be ushered up to bed.

About nine p.m. Dad would tune into Lord Haw-Haws 'Germany calling, Germany calling'. This was a German propaganda programme aimed at demoralising the British people. The broadcast always began with a piece of classical music, Beethoven's Symphony No. 9 then 'Lord Haw-Haw' (William Joyce) speaking in an upper class English accent and tell listeners about our merchant ships lost to German U-boats that week. His gloating voice would go on and telling of the casualties and desolation that had been inflicted by the Luftwaffe on our major cities. During the early part of the war there was a news blackout on the bombings of our cities which caused a great deal of anger and distress amongst the population, especially those who knew what had happened. With news hard to come by people began to listen to the 'Germany calling, Germany calling', broadcasts, and many believed them. It was said that half the population of Britain listened to these illicit broadcasts. One evening when I went downstairs to the lavatory I dawdled so I could listen to the 'Germany calling' broadcast, but I was forbidden to talk about it to anyone. Listening to 'Lord Haw-Haw' was deemed as treacherous, and talking about it helped to spread rumours and persuade people the war was going badly and invasion was imminent. It was said that German U-boats were being refuelled in Southern Ireland. "Divide and conquer." said Dad and although he wasn't fond of the Irish, he reminded us about the Irish lads in the Crescent who were in the Forces.

After listening to the 'Germany calling' broadcast I began to take an interest in the news. The Government had realised that having a news blackout had simply driven people to listen to the German propaganda, so reporting restrictions were relaxed. I noticed that at the end of every B.B.C. news broadcast, usually after the weather forecast, a list of strange and nonsensically obscure messages were read out. These messages meant nothing to me, but to the people in enemy territory waiting for the messages they could mean the difference between life and death.

There were no books in our house so as I grew older I began to read Dad's newspaper, taking an interest in articles about the war. I remember a statement being issued by the German High Command which claimed that; 'The aircraft engine works at Leyland, north of

Liverpool, and also hangars and planes on the ground have been destroyed'.

This puzzled me as whilst I knew they made lots of different engines at the Motors, and lots of the other factories made bits for planes, we absolutely had no planes or hangars in Leyland at all, and anyway, nothing in Leyland had been destroyed, I'm sure someone would have noticed!

This was all part of the propaganda war which of course was played out by both sides. In turn, our Government would make comical light at some of the air raids; like a story about a bombing raid on a hen house killing a couple of chickens. But when the Luftwaffe made night raids on our part of Lancashire, we huddled in fear under our kitchen table, as the planes would drop flares in an attempt to locate the R.O.F. factory at Euxton.

Chapter Ten

During WWII the Government encouraged the population who had gardens, allotments and even window boxes to grow their own fruit and vegetables. 'Dig for Victory' posters appeared on hoardings, noticeboards and public transport all over the country. The propaganda was relentless and it became a crime, punishable by prison, to waste food. Even village greens and more or less every bit of grass that wasn't being used for farming or airfields was turned over to food production. Councils up and down the country relaxed planning laws to enable people to keep livestock in their back gardens. People kept hens, rabbits and geese in order to supplement their diet. Anything you had spare was used to barter for other goods, and on the whole it worked rather well.

One of the best bits of propaganda was the drive to eat carrots, which all of a sudden the country had loads of, and were a good source of sugar which few other available foods contained. The Government wanted to keep the fact we had invented radar as secret as possible, so they claimed that the reason the RAF were shooting down so many planes was because the pilots ate carrots, and they helped you see at night. Posters were then put up all over the place, saying just that, trying to encourage people to eat more of the surplus carrots. And it didn't end there, there were leaflets with carrot based recipes, the only one of which anyone liked was carrot cake, and Walt Disney was even commissioned to come up with a whole family of cartoon carrots, but the only cartoon carrot I remember from the war was the one Bugs Bunny was always chewing.

The Government then allowed the populace to form Pig Clubs. Edgehill Crescent didn't have a Pig Club, but Broadfield Drive did. The Pig Clubs worked like this; a group of people would club together and buy a pig. The pig would be suitably housed somewhere, then everyone belonging to the club would feed the pig with scraps from their kitchen table until it was ready for slaughtering. The Broadfield's pig was penned at Cherry Ripes farm, but the farmer didn't do the slaughtering, that was the job for members of the Club. Mr. Johnson who lived in Broadfields was one of the members of the Club who took on that task. When the pig was killed it was jointed and shared out amongst the Club members. As no one wanted the trotters, Mr. Johnson's wife Hetty brought them round to our house for Mam to turn into brawn[7] for Dad's bagging.

Hetty was a regular visitor to our house as was her daughter Dorothy, a rather portly girl with a fondness for chips. Dad wouldn't have a chip pan in the house, I think he had a relative who died in a chip pan fire, so on Saturday nights when Dad was away for the weekend, Dorothy would cycle round to our house with a chip pan full of cold, white lard, set solid from the last time it was used, on the handlebars of her bike. Mam would make a big pan full of chips for us all, and then we would sit around a warm fire eating chip butties listening to the wireless. There still wasn't much news to listen to a lot

---

[7] Brawn is pig trotters, boiled with a little chopped meat added, bones removed and left to set in its own jelly in the pantry.

of the time, but we did get I.T.M.A (It's That Man Again), a comedy programme starring Tommy Handley which we all enjoyed. If the Saturday night play wasn't too scary, we were allowed to listen to that. My favourite programmes at that time were the big dance bands, who played the latest popular tunes.

Music played an important part in the war effort, the Government had found that workers doing ten hour shifts became exhausted well before the end of their shifts, so they commissioned the B.B.C. to broadcast a mid-afternoon programme called 'Music While You Work' which was relayed to factories on war production. It was so successful in increasing production that an evening programme was introduced. Music lifted the spirits of the workers who would sing and work to the rhythm of the catchy tunes. Continuous music was then piped to most of the factories on war work throughout the country. In the larger factories big bands such as 'Geraldo and His Orchestra' or the 'B.B.C. Light Orchestra' played in the canteens for workers on late shifts. Sometimes workers would muster up enough energy to dance. My favourite song at that time was 'Yes My Darling Daughter' which I sang continuously on my way to school.

Music While You Work carried on for the duration of the war right until it was ended in 1967, when the pirate radio stations finally taught the B.B.C. that music and tastes had changed and they had to start broadcasting this new-fangled 'pop' music!

Chapter Eleven

Saturday was washday and usually the day that Mam baked. Mam was a good baker, well organised and able to adapt to the ingredients the war left her with. On Friday nights the fire in the living room would be banked up with potato peelings and a little coal; this would smoulder all night heating the back boiler and kitchen range ready for the following day, Early Saturday morning Mam would fill the washing boiler with the already warm water and boil the dirty clothes. Whilst the clothes were boiling she would bake meat pies, jam tarts, and if any of the neighbour's geese had strayed into our back garden and laid an egg or two we had custard pies. Any pastry left over would be made into Chorley cakes[8] for Dad to take with him in his bagging box on Monday morning. If we had been scrumping in Farmer Forester's orchards, or we'd been blackberry picking we had blackberry or apple pies as well. Whilst Mam's baking was cooking in the kitchen range I helped her to poss[9] the clothes in the boiler with the Persil. After a good possing, the clothes were then taken out of the boiler and scrubbed on the kitchen table with the Fairy soap. Then, after a good rinsing they were taken outside and put through a mangle by the back door and pegged on the line to dry. Two flat

---

[8] Chorley cakes are not unlike the cake from the neighbouring town of Eccles, but not as posh. Whilst Eccles cakes are made by putting raisins into puff-pastry, Chorley cakes are raisins inside leftover pastry.

[9] Possing: Agitating clothes in water.

irons would be on the kitchen range ready to use; after the ironing had been done we would fold the clothes neatly put them on the clothes maiden, in the kitchen and hoist it up to the ceiling with pulleys. The clothes stayed on the clothes maiden because we didn't have wardrobes or drawers to keep them in. We hadn't a lot of clothes just our school clothes and best clothes which we only wore at weekends, but even so the whole operation took most of the day.

When we had finished, we would all sit down in a lovely warm kitchen and have tea. Mam worked hard and there was no one more pleased than me when she eventually got a basic washing machine, and shortly after buying the washing machine she bought a second hand cooker. This caused a row between my parents. My dad thought it was a waste of money as we had a good kitchen range, but as Mam pointed out the only way she could boil a kettle quickly was on a gas ring under the kitchen sink which she thought was dangerous. The rubber piping on the gas ring was always coming loose and what with Dad smoking, Mam thought it'd be him who would end up blowing us up, not the Germans.

One weekend Dad came home with a couple of rabbits which he had bought on the black market. Mam was pleased because the rabbits had already been skinned and that was a job she detested. She popped the rabbits into a pan with a few carrots and onions but as the rabbits cooked she complained to Dad the stew didn't smell right. Dad tasted the meat, did a bit of sputtering, and then the whole lot went into the councils pig bin. Dad suspected he had been sold cats. Hopefully this was not what had happened to our moggy! In future rabbits and fowl were bought with fur and feathers still attached!

When Mrs. B. walked in, grumbling about the food shortages, my darling brother piped up: "Why don't you go to the same market as my mam?"

"What market is that, Melvin?" she asked

"The black market!" Mel replied.

I can't remember if this was met with laughter or a sharp outburst of *"Melvin!"* from my parents, but it was a good job it was Mrs. B. he was talking to, because buying from the black market was something to be frowned on even though most people did.

Later that week we had unexpected visitors. My mam apologised because she was unable to make them a cup of tea.

"But, Mam, you have a caddy full of tea," I said.

I opened the dresser door and took out a full caddy of tea, and when the kettle was boiled I brewed the 'tea'. It was too weak to crawl out of the pot. 'Water bewitched, tea begrudged', as my grandma would say.

What I thought was tea, was actually a caddy full of poppy seeds that Dad had collected from the corn fields on his way home from work. He had intended to scatter the poppy seeds in the front garden in memory of his brother Bill who had died on the Somme.

Chapter Twelve

Although Japan had first invaded China in 1937, we only realised the Japanese were in the war on the wrong side after the bombing of Pearl Harbour, which sent shock waves throughout the British Isles. The threat of an invasion by the Japanese held a far greater fear to the British people than one by the Germans.

One day Mam solemnly declared, "If the Japanese set foot on these shores I will kill us all."

Quite calmly she said she would do this rather than let us fall into the hands of the Japanese. Mass suicide had already been talked about because of the threat of German invasion, however by the autumn of 1940 all that talk of suicide had abated. How was Mam going to kill us? We didn't own a gun, but like most of our neighbours in the Crescent we did now have a gas oven, but the most talked about method was poison.

"Where would Mam get the poison?" I asked my dad.

Silently he looked up at the ceiling. There, hanging from a light bulb in the kitchen was a flycatcher covered in dead flies. Most of our neighbours had these horrible arsenic fly catchers hanging from their ceiling. Some even had two. Ours disappeared overnight, as did our neighbours'. Having instant death hanging from the ceiling like 'Damocles 'sword' was a 'temptation too far' for most husbands.

The bombing of Pearl Harbour had finally brought the Americans into the war, and in the spring of 1942 a million American soldiers landed on our shores under the code name 'Bolero'. The soldiers were dispersed through the British Isles to provide security to strategic areas. The Royal Ordnance Factory at Euxton was now flanked by two American bases one on either side. One was in Mounsey Street in Bamber Bridge, and another much larger base was situated off the Southport Road between Euxton and Chorley. There was one minor problem with it, named after the nearby brook; the road it was actually on was called German Lane. This soon became Washington Lane and the base was 'Washington Hall'.

Also on the Southport Road was a hostel called the 'Woodlands'. Woodlands housed mainly key workers and young men who had been drafted into the area for the duration of the war. Two miles away at Euxton there was another hostel called 'The Highways' which had recently been opened by Mrs. Churchill the Prime Minister's wife. The Highways accommodated nearly two thousand young women between the ages of eighteen to thirty years of age, most of whom had been compulsory called up to work in the mills and the munitions factory at Euxton. These young women came from all walks of life and despite the social differences, a great spirit of camaraderie developed between them. Aunt Irene had been called up to work at Euxton, but being a local, she lived at home.

Whilst it was called a 'hostel', Highways was really a compact village boasting a medical centre, a post office, a cinema, and a dance hall. Church services were held each Sunday and dances most Saturdays; these dances proved to be both popular with the locals and with the Americans stationed in the area, who quite naturally gravitated to Highways. Aunt Irene gravitated to a GI named Andy. It will come as little surprise to know that

71

it was said that many of the young women who sailed to America as war brides in 1946 had met their husbands at Highways.

The girls working at the Euxton munitions factory worked under dangerous conditions, not only from the threat of air raids, but from freak accidents in the factory as Nora, who would later become my sister-in-law explained to me, "We had to fill shells with powder and when the box was full two of us had to carry it to another room. Every time we made the journey we had to have another girl walking in front of us with a red flag. One day the box we were carrying exploded; it blew one of the girl's hands off. It was static electricity that caused it".

Like my mam had, the girls who worked with cordite for any length of time became jaundiced and turned yellow. These workers would be given time off to recuperate, with one worker recalling, "We had to convalesce on a diet of raw fish. Ugh!"

Aunt Irene was working at Euxton when she became very ill with cordite poisoning and she was hospitalised at Chorley Hospital where her sister Mildred was now working as a student nurse.

Irene made the natural 'mistake' of calling her own sister Mildred, who amazingly gave her this curt reply, "You address me as Nurse Goodman."

That didn't go down very well with my Aunt Irene who was completely shocked by this unexpected response, but of course this was a time in history when Matron ruled the hospital with a rod of iron, discipline was strict and distance and decorum had to be maintained, even when it was your own sister laid in the bed in front of you. It was a time when nurses had to win the cuffs and belts of their uniform in order to progress. It was also a time when cleanliness took the absolute priority and bugs would never get the chance to close wards.

Cordite poisoning was blamed for an epidemic of impetigo that was sweeping the area at the time, but the main fear for the workers at the munitions factory was of course the danger of air raids.

When enemy planes were spotted flying towards the area an elaborate camouflage system, which might seem futuristic even now, would swing into action. Much of the factory was underground, with the sprawling flat-roofed buildings and the gantries surrounding them that were designed to deflect bombs heavily camouflaged. But as an extra measure to not give anything away to the enemy above as to the location of the factory, the outer gate would slam shut entombing everyone who worked there, and once the gate was sealed water was released into the compound, turning the surrounding area into a lake, which would throw the Germans off. It was said that if anyone was caught outside the factory when this happened, they would be shot if they ran away, as the Germans would instantly wonder what they were running from. Although I was told this after the war, I never got close enough to the factory to prove it with my own eyes, but this would explain why it was so difficult to find.

Like the factory buildings, the houses surrounding Euxton were also part of the camouflage, with most of them having flat roofs which the occupants were encouraged to grow vegetables and flowers on. Whenever we visited my grandparents in Chorley the bus we caught went past these houses, and I thought these houses with plants growing out of the roofs looked incredibly funny until I got ticked off by my mam. She told me that the people living in those houses cultivated their roofs so they looked like allotments from the air, camouflaging them to confuse the Germans and stop Euxton from being bombed.

One day, when a stray bomb landed not too far away from Euxton, like the one that fell outside our school, it failed to go off. When it was made safe, the shell was placed outside the factory gates, as a reminder not just of the devastation that one bomb could do, but as a symbol of pride that so many German bombs had failed to explode, whilst everyone who worked at Euxton were certain all of the bombs that they made would detonate on their targets.

Like everyone who had been called up to work at Euxton, Post War Credits were taken out of my aunt's wages after her weekly income tax had been deducted. On the face of it, it was a temporary loan to the Government to help pay for the war, with Post War Credits to be paid back after the war 'or as soon as maybe'.

A lot of people actually saw this as a good thing, as whilst the PWCs were clearly an extra tax, if you worked at a place like Euxton, having money during the war wasn't the biggest issue, having something to be able to spend it on was. So the idea that there would be a big payout when the war, and rationing, had ended, seemed like a great idea. It seemed to some that it was like putting money into a bank that could only fail if we lost the war. Many were more sceptical, doubting they would ever see their money again.

When Aunt Irene got out of hospital, she had been deemed to have got so ill that she would not be sent back to Euxton, but instead went to work in the textile mill.

***

Later in the war the factory at Euxton would become the home of Barnes Wallis's bouncing bomb. After much development and testing, the bombs inflicted colossal damage, at a high cost, on the dams in the Ruhr Valley in 1943.

Chapter Thirteen

On 22nd April 1942 the Ministry of Food announced that a ration of oranges was to be distributed to everyone in the country. The Crescent waited in anticipation for the precious, and for many of us children never seen, fruit to arrive at the farm. Days went by and there was no sign of this mystical promised fruit. Then one day my pest of a brother, bless him, managed for once to do something right. It happened like this. There was a rumour going around the Crescent that the farm had received a consignment of oranges. All efforts by Mrs. B. to glean any information from the farm about the precious cargo, proved fruitless. Ever the cynic, Dad thought the whole thing was just a ruse to drum up custom to buy overpriced vegetables and burnt ice cream[10]. Mam chastised him, because if he dug for victory like some of the men in the street she wouldn't have to buy vegetables from the farm.

"The soil is too sandy," Dad groaned.

"It's all right for carrots," she snapped back.

Apart from when Mel and I had tried to make a shelter, which Dad had never finished, our garden had never been dug over, it was a jungle of weeds, but our neighbour's poultry loved it. As a result we got the odd egg, much to the annoyance of Mrs. B. But to be fair Dad did his best, consistently getting the odd gallon of petrol

---

[10] Sometimes, when Cherry Ripes tried to make ice-cream they would burn the milk when boiling it. Or maybe they decided after burning milk the only thing they could do with it was make ice cream?

for the mobile butcher, at great risk I might add, but anyway let's get back to those oranges. Everyone was too busy arguing to notice that Mel had disappeared; puzzled I went looking for him. I was just in time to see the tail end of him, as he vanished through a hole in the fence at the bottom of our garden. I watched open mouthed as he charged over Cherry Ripes field, then with the skill of an athlete he cleared the stile at the bottom of Broadfield Drive, and ran hell for leather up to the farm. Mel had never tasted a real orange; he'd never even seen an orange, so if there was any about he would find them. About half an hour later Mrs. B popped her head around our kitchen door to inform us that the cart from the farm was at the top of the Crescent.

Excitedly we all ran out and formed an orderly queue at the bottom of the Crescent; we could tell from the disappointed groans coming from the top of the Crescent that there were no oranges. The cart eventually arrived outside our house where the horse was given a drink of water, and then after the customers had been served, the cart would turn around and the horse would gallop up the street to Broadfield Drive, the last stop before going back to the farm.

Well, that's what usually happened, but not today!

Mam and Mrs. B bought their usual week's vegetables then they asked about the oranges. Cherry Ripe's daughter-in-law snapped at them. "I am fed up with telling you people." Her voice now raised, "We have no oranges!"

"Oh yes you have!" shouted my long lost brother, who with the stealth and patience to wait for the perfect moment that any spy or commando would be proud of, had seen what had happened at the farm, and now he was

ready to complete his mission. Before anyone could stop him, Melvin dived under the cart, opened a secret compartment, and out fell oranges! Lovely sunshiny oranges! They rolled under the cart, through the horse's legs and down the Crescent. Delighted children and adults scrambled to grab a precious orange, with possession being nine parts of the law. The luckless daughter-in-law had no choice but to let the customers in Edgehill have their share of the fruit, haplessly trying to charge the people she saw running off with them. Instead of the oranges being for the favoured few in Broadfield who could afford to pay the extra, Melvin had distributed them here.

Melvin was a hero.

Chapter Fourteen

Dad had been away for some time with his wagon when a letter came for Mam, and as she wasn't in I placed it on the mantelpiece to wait for her return. It was only the second letter that Mam had received since we came to live in the Crescent.

The first letter had been from her friend 'Aunt Polly', who was my godmother, to inform Mam that she was now living in Coventry in a place called Primrose Hill, which sounded to me like it must be a beautiful idyllic place. Aunt Polly had gone with a doctor friend to the city in 1940. She had been a cook at Chorley Hospital when Mam, pregnant with me, had been admitted to the Hospital after falling off a stool when putting up curtains in the living room. I was born by caesarean section and was not expected to live so I was immediately christened in the hospital chapel that's how my Aunt Polly became my godmother and not a member of the family, because she was just there at the time. In those days when such circumstances arose it was not unusual for the baby boy to be named after the king and the girl after the queen. It may have been at this emergency christening I was named Mary, if I was, Dad soon changed it as Mary with its religious connotations was not a name Dad was fond of. Mam was very ill after my birth the doctor's said it was a combination of poor diet and grinding poverty. When the doctor's became concerned about mams condition they asked dad if they could use a new drug, as mam wasn't getting any better dad gave his permission.

A week later she was well enough to be moved to the main ward, where she found her sister Marshall who had also had a baby girl who had been called May. When mam was well enough to go home the doctors presented her with a big box of chocolates for her bravery, after the chocolates had been eaten the box was used as a safe to keep important documents in. During a top to bottom spring clean I came across the box and that's when mam sat me down and told me this story.

After that one letter from Aunt Polly Mam never heard from her again, but she never stopped hoping that one day she would get a second letter from Coventry. The reality was that after November 1940, Primrose Hill in Coventry was most certainly not a beautiful idyllic place.

Mam opened the letter as soon as she came into the house; it was from my dad inviting us to spend a few days with him in Wigton where he was now working. With our gas masks, identity cards, ration books and refreshments to fortify us for the long journey we boarded the Carlisle train. We found ourselves in a carriage with a young neighbour called Mary who was going to stay with relatives in Scotland. Mary and Mam spent the journey chatting while Mel and I read and re-read a comic we had managed to swop for some steelies. I was glad this was a train with blackout blinds, because in the war some train carriages had the windows painted black, so you couldn't see out of the windows, night or day.

On arriving at Wigton, Dad was waiting on the platform, then after a bit of hugging and kissing he took us in his wagon to his lodgings in the town. We were to stay with a policeman and his wife who had two children, a boy and girl of similar ages to us. During the week Dad would take us out in his wagon and leave us in the lovely countryside surrounding Wigton where we would spend the day exploring and watching Lancaster Bombers fly over. At a pre-arranged spot Dad would pick us up and take us back to his lodgings where we would have tea with our hosts and their family. After tea we would play in the street with their children until it was time for bed. At the end of the week Mam went into Wigton with Dad to have a look round the town. They liked the town and Dad particularly liked the fountain in the town centre, a bit of triviality that was almost pretending there was no war.

We didn't go into town. Instead, Mel and I went to a backstreet cinema with our two new friends. We didn't see a Tarzan or a Bud Abbot and Lou Costello film; we saw 'The Night Has Eyes', a creepy film about a schoolteacher who goes missing in bog country. When her friend finds her skeleton in the attic of a lonely farmhouse suspicion falls on the son of the house who has post-traumatic stress from his war experiences. The real culprit ends up falling in the bog. I can still remember the hands as they slowly disappeared in the bog just to be replaced by bubbles. It was that film, not the war, that gave me nightmares for years to come.

Chapter Fifteen

In the winter of 1942 the street was ravaged with a flu epidemic; nearly every house in the street had someone ill. At the top of the street a friend's brother was so ill he had been taken to hospital, but the little lad died. His mam used the family's clothing coupons so that she could bring her son home in a new suit. His name was Eric, he was eleven-years-old, and his new suit became his shroud.

Almost everyone had been ill, because we were all so run down by rationing and doing so much. Mam had been to the doctors and had been told she was anaemic. This diagnosis had been followed by the medical recommendation that she should drink Guinness. Melvin had been so ill that his pillow was covered in blood from all his nosebleeds.

It was a bitter cold November morning and I was enjoying my hot pobs, when Mrs. B breezed into the kitchen. "Tell you what Nellie I haven't seen little Eva for a while, have the twins said anything about their Mam?"

Mam shook her head. "No they haven't, and come to think about it I haven't seen her about either, what with Melvin being ill with the flu I haven't had time for anything else."

They both looked at each other strangely then went into a whispered huddle. I was unceremoniously hustled out of the house to catch the school bus at Earnshaw Bridge, now I had moved on to Fox Lane Junior. Every morning I would go to the bus stop which was just in front of my old school. There I would board a double-decker bus to the other side of town. The boys would go on the top deck, and the girls on the bottom, coming back at four p.m.

When I arrived home that afternoon the street was abound with gossip. Mam and Mrs. B had broken into little Eva's house. They had found her so ill that they called for a doctor who immediately sent for an ambulance. Eva was taken to hospital, gravely ill with pneumonia. What the street didn't know and would never know, at least not from Mam or Mrs. B, was that when they broke into the house they found their friend in bed under a pile of coats. There was no shame in this if truth was known, half the street went to sleep under coats, and that included us.

A few days later on another bitter cold wet day, there was a timid knock at the front door. As I was coming down the stairs at the time I answered the door. Maurice stood on the doorstep silent, shaking, rivulets of tears streaking down his grubby face, but before I had time to talk to him my mam brushed past me and put her arms around him and took him into the warm front room. There he sat in the hearth with his arms wrapped around his legs, steam billowing from his damp clothes, silently sobbing as he rocked to and fro. Then before I could ask him what was the matter Mam walked in with a bowl of steaming hot pobs and once again I was packed off to school.

When I returned from school that afternoon Mam told me that the twins' mam had died and I wouldn't be seeing my friends for a while, as they had gone to stay with their grandparents in Blackburn. As was the custom Maggie from number 40 went round the Crescent knocking on doors collecting money for a wreath, then before she handed it over to the bereaved family, she took it round to all those who had contributed so they could see it. It seemed to me at the time that she spent all that winter knocking on doors collecting money for wreaths. Unlike the other funerals Eva's cortege didn't go from her home, but from her parent's house in Blackburn, but as a mark of respect her friends and neighbours drew their curtains anyway. Little Eva was a proud, gentle lady who would be sadly missed by her friends.

Some months later a troubled Mr. Dean came over to see my parents. He said he'd had a visit from the authorities about Maurice and Dennis and they had advised him to place the lads into an orphanage until they were ready for work. Mr. Dean was reluctant to let the lads go and the lads didn't want to go. But Dad thought the authorities were right. "The lads are alright now because they come over here after school and Nellie keeps an eye on them, but what's going to happen during the summer holidays when they have to fend for themselves while you are at work? You don't want them getting into trouble like some of the kids in the street, Eva wouldn't have wanted that."

Later, Dad talked to the lads. "Look at it this way; you will be going to boarding school just like the rich kids. You will be able to visit your dad during the holidays, and you may be able to visit your grandparents as well."

Dad's advice was taken and the boys spent the next few years in Preston. When they did come home in the holidays they got ribbed by the lads in the street because they were still in short trousers whilst the boys in the Crescent of a similar age had progressed to long ones.

Mel had sidled off to Bannister Brook with Bonzo and the older boys. Mam sighed; "Bring him back before he falls in the brook, Mavis, will you?"

The last time he fell in the brook Mam had to rinse out his smelly clothes and put them in the oven to dry. Because he had nothing to change into he had to wear one of my dresses, so he spent the whole afternoon growling and pacing about like a caged lion. Mam thought that would cure him of brook jumping, but it didn't.

I ran over the fields and found a group of lads in a huddle by the water's edge. They were laughing at something that one of the older boys was holding, so I moved closer to see what they were laughing at. One of the lads was blowing a frog up through a reed shoved up its bum. Incensed with rage I charged into the group, grabbed the unfortunate frog, and threw it as far as I could upstream, then I grabbed my brother and ran, but not before I got clobbered by one of the lads. Bonzo was useless. She saw me throw the frog and thought it was a game and charged upstream to retrieve it. She came back so proud that she'd managed to retrieve such a tricky item, and like any dog would she had 'throw it again, throw it again' written all over her face, but given that the boys were now laughing instead of trying to hit me, I couldn't be too angry.

* * *

During the spring, summer and autumn months the brook was a magnet to all the children from all streets. In the autumn we would go brook jumping. In the spring, clutching our jam jars, we would go down to the brook to catch tadpoles and sticklebacks or go bird nesting in the hedges in the surrounding fields. This was a pursuit frowned upon by our parents, but when Mel came home with two different coloured eggs which he had found in one nest, things changed a little. It was explained to him that the big brown coloured egg was a cuckoo and the little blue one was a hedge sparrow. Mam told him that the cuckoo egg usually hatched before the sparrow's. When that happened, the cuckoo would then turf all the little sparrow's eggs out of the nest so the mother sparrow would spend all her time feeding the big lazy cuckoo until she was exhausted. After this revelation it was hunt the cuckoo egg. When Mel found a little sparrow that had been booted out of its nest by a cuckoo he reverently buried it in our back garden.

In the summer months during the school holidays, we would swim in Bannister Brook. This was of great concern to our parents because the brook travelled through most of the factories that were on war work. After which it went under the road on School Lane, surfacing onto Farmer Forester's land. After that it meandered into Cherry Ripes field where it cascaded over a waterfall that divided the two farmers' land. More often than not dead calves would be stuck on the waterfall ready to fall down into our little nook below, but they were soon moved by Farmer Forester's workers.

The nook was a favourite spot for all the children of the streets. We would swing on ropes from trees whooping as we fell into the water below all happily playing together. One summer, late into the war all that came to an end. It wasn't the soldiers or the farmers that stopped us playing in the fields, it was the influence the war was having on us. One weekend the lads from the three streets gathered in gangs on both sides of the brook shouting abuse at each other. Things hotted up a level when they progressed to hurling stones, next they started to use catapults, but when one of the lads from Broadfield produced an air rifle the war games had escalated into real danger. After that incident most of the parents banned their children from playing in the fields.

Chapter Sixteen

The previous tenants of our house had painted all the downstairs white, but now it was getting a little grubby and Mam thought it was time for a change. The white walls made everyone feel cold, Mel and I agreed with her, and Mam decided she wanted the living room painting a nice shade of green. Dad said he knew where he could lay his hands on some green paint. A few weeks later, true to his word, he came home at the weekend with two gallons of green paint. The colour of the paint was Burma green, not quite the colour that Mam had in mind. "It looks more like camouflage paint" Mam moaned, "it will make the place look like a jungle."

"Beggars can't be choosers," Dad retorted, because of course it *was* camouflage paint that had probably found its way from the back of his wagon to the cab, *"So you'll have to make the best of it."*

Still grumbling about the awful colour we all began to paint the walls. After a while we stood back to admire our handiwork. It was far worse than we could possibly have imagined. It was even worse than our school shelters.

Then Mam had an idea. "There's a tin of whitewash in the pantry left by the last tenants. We could use some of that to make it lighter."

The tin of paint was brought into the front room and mixed with the green, and once again we all began to paint the walls. When we had finished we surveyed our handiwork. While not everyone agreed whether it was better or worse, we all agreed that it was still awful.

"It'll dry lighter," said Dad, hopefully.

Then Mam had another bright idea. Determined to make the best of it, she took some powdered rouge out of her handbag which she mixed with remains of the whitewash, producing a lovely shade of pink. Then she went to her sewing box, took the needles and pins out of a darning mushroom, and covered it with a piece of lace. When the lace was secure the mushroom was dipped in the pink paint and stippled onto the dark green walls. Mel, had been doing potato stippling at school that week and had brought his potato home, joined in enthusiastically.

Dad was so impressed he let Mel carry on then we found some dolly blue and yellow curtain die which we also stippled on the walls. Dad brought a ladder in so he could do a frieze along the picture rail; I stood on the table putting pink squiggles in between all the stippling. We were dabbing it here and dabbing it there. By the time we had finished we were all covered in paint, but we all had to agree the walls looked quite nice. We had done a good job.

The following week Dad brought home some lovely cream paint which he painted on the kitchen walls. The trouble with this paint was it was gloss paint, meant for wood, so when Mam lit the copper boiler the next washday, condensation ran down the walls forming puddles on the kitchen floor. Needless to say, the rest of the house wasn't decorated until after the war.

Chapter Seventeen

Once a fortnight the 'Parched Pea[11] King' would trundle his barrow into Edgehill ringing his bell, shouting: *"Parch Peas! Parch Peas! Hot Parch Peas!"* He would make a stop at the top of the street sell a few bags of hot parched peas then trundle his way halfway down the street, where he would leave his barrow outside a neighbour's house opposite whilst he had a cup of tea. After about ten minutes he would re-appear ringing his bell shouting, "Parch Peas, Hot Parch Peas." It so happened that the sons of the house that he stopped at decided to play a nasty trick on him. While he was in the house enjoying a cup of tea and a chat, they crept around the back of the house to the rabbit hutches. They gathered the day's droppings and emptied the smelly lot into his barrow of parched peas. That was the last time the Parched Pea King visited our street. However, he did have a safer pitch outside the Saturday morning flea pit.

'The Palace', if there could ever be a more undeserved name, is where he would sell his hot parched peas to the cinema queue on Saturday mornings. Usually the parched peas would end up in pea shooters and used as ammunition by rival gangs of lads inside until the cartoons came on. The cartoons were usually followed by the Pathe Newsreel. When the news was bad we would boo, but when the news was good we would all cheer. On

---

[11] 'Parched Peas' are normal garden peas that have been roasted. In this case, in a mobile oven similar to the larger ovens used today for roasted chestnuts and roasted potatoes.

this particular Saturday, my friend Doreen from number 34 and I went to the Palace Cinema, and the only seats we could find were next to a row of young men of what we called then 'mixed abilities'.

These young men and their carers walked to the cinema every Saturday from a residential home just outside Leyland. They all sat in one row, and were generally very well behaved. Everything was fine until halfway through the main feature; then I felt a nudge. *"Look,"* said a voice. I looked in the dark, but I couldn't see a thing. It happened again and still I couldn't see anything. Doreen asked me what was going on. When I told her she said, *"If it happens again give me a nudge."*

Moments later I nudged her. "Oh heavens," my worldly friend shrieked. "Are you stupid or something, he's showing you his sausage!"

With that she grabbed my hand and yanked me out of my seat, and we fled the cinema.

That wasn't the only sausage I saw that year. I was invited to a birthday party by a school friend. Halfway through the party I was asked to go into the kitchen to fetch some sandwiches and was followed into the kitchen by my friend's older brother. He got me into a corner by the pantry door, and then he plonked his sausage on the kitchen table. He was obviously very proud of it, but I am afraid I just laughed, before I wriggled free and fled through the back door. At school the following day, my friend asked me why I had left so suddenly. Quite truthfully I told her that 'I felt sick'. I knew my friend's brother had been called up for the Army and I probably wouldn't be seeing him again for years, so I kept the incident to myself. Anyway who would believe me?

Chapter Eighteen

Aunt Irene and Andy

I saw a lot of my Aunt Irene during the war. Whilst she had been conscripted to go into the factories, the hostels were for those from other parts of the country, but she still lived with Grandma and Grandad, and they, or at least Grandma, wasn't over enamoured at her daughter going out with a 'Dam Yank'. Like most parents in the North West she was worried about her daughter falling pregnant and being deserted or widowed by her American boyfriend. The Yanks very much had a 'good time' reputation, and the phrase 'Overpaid, Over-sexed, and Over here' started being repeated up and down the country.

It was also of course true that some girls did fall pregnant. The English girls, many of them like the conscripts at Highways, were away from home for the first time in their lives and were complete innocents as far as birth control was concerned, and were easy prey for the brash Americans. On the whole, there were many long lasting friendships which lead to marriage, but there were some GIs who were complete bastards.

It turned out that posted on the noticeboard in the mess at Washington Hall were details of the sexual health of some of what the Americans considered to be the 'easier' British girls. When this got out, the locals got very angry as they saw their girls as victims who had been innocent until they had been given diseases by the American soldiers. All indiscretions and criminal acts were dealt with quietly and swiftly by the Americans themselves.

My parents made my aunt's American boyfriend welcome. As far as they were concerned he was a lad thousands of miles away from home.

Aunt Mildred. Born 15th August 1923

Aunt Mildred was a remote figure in my life. She was the only one of my grandma's children who got into grammar school, because she was educated she was able to escape being sent into the mills by her parents. Going to grammar school enabled children to move beyond the class and poverty they were born into. Mildred literally now lived in a different world to us.

During the Liverpool blitz Mildred was a nurse at St. Helen's Hospital near Liverpool, where she met the American sergeant who would later become her husband. In the winter of 1942 he visited the hospital to pick up supplies of penicillin and use the sterilizing facilities. Mildred always said it was love at first sight. When Otto asked for my Aunt's hand in marriage my grandparents opposed it, which would have meant they could not get married as then parents had to give permission for the children to marry if they were under twenty-one.

They were uneasy because Otto was older and more 'experienced' than my aunt and Grandma thought he might have a wife back in the States. Eventually they gave their blessing. Otto and Mildred were married on the 20th September 1943 at Chorley Registrar Office a year after they had met.

Irene and Andy were not so lucky. I can't imagine that it was because Grandma didn't like Andy. There wasn't the big age gap there had been between Mildred and Otto, but she never gave them permission to marry, so they had to wait until Irene was twenty-one. Most likely she had refused because Irene was still living at home with Grandma and Grandad and they relied on her wages and ration coupons coming into the household, but I simply don't know, that was what I thought at the time.

Irene Goodman, aged twenty-two, of Harrison Road, Chorley, Lancashire, married Andrew Dunn of Nebraska Avenue, St. Louis, Missouri, America at Chorley Registrar on April 23rd 1944.

After Irene and Andy married they moved into a flat above a butcher's shop in Steely Lane in Chorley. Andy of course would only be there when he had leave, but had decided that was better than making Irene endure the inevitable ogling and seedy approaches she would have faced on a daily basis on the base. One time when Andy had leave and my aunt was working, he was given the job of picking up her week's rations from the shop where she was registered. He went to the shop gave the shopkeeper the list his wife had given him. The shopkeeper weighed everything carefully, put the groceries on the counter, and waited patiently for payment.

"I asked for all her weekly rations, not for just one day!"

Resisting the temptation to laugh, or roll his eyes, the shopkeeper calmly explained that these were her weekly rations. Andy exploded!

"How am I going to get my wife through a medical to go to America if she has to live on these starvation rations?"

This incident was a rude awakening to Andy about the hardships that the British people had to endure not only from the bombings, but from rationing. If it were it not for the Land Army and the sacrifices of the brave Merchant Seamen who ran the gauntlet of U-boats every day, the nation would not be hungry, but starving.

Whenever American soldiers were invited into the homes of the local population, their hosts would put on a spread for their guests that would have probably used up almost all the families' rations for the entire week. On the whole, the Americans seemed to be ignorant of the generosity of their hosts, as they ate better back at barracks than anyone else in the country.

Uncle Andy's encounter with the shopkeeper brought a massively positive outcome for us. He'd always brought the odd bit of something when he had come around before, but now whenever he came to visit us he would come laden down with tins of pineapple, peaches, Spam, jam and cigarettes for Dad, and American 'candy' for us. Mel and I didn't care for the 'candy', we would have preferred proper sweets, because it always seemed to taste like medicine, but it was great for swapping for things like comics. One day, much to Mam's, delight he even brought some parachute silk which she had made into cami-knickers for herself and Irene by a delighted dressmaker, who was paid in kind for her expertise, getting to keep the rest of the silk.

Chapter Nineteen

Aunt Mildred was a rare visitor to our house, but on the one occasion she did visit it proved to be a blessing. I had been feeling poorly for some time with earache. I had rather a large lump at the back of my left ear which was getting bigger as the days went by. It was causing me a great deal of pain, and causing my mam concern. After a visit to our surgery the doctor advised her to poultice the affected area.

I upset my mam by screeching each time she did. She was just about to administer a poultice for the third time when an angel in the form of my Aunt Mildred walked through the door. After she had examined me I was on my way to Chorley Hospital, and went straight into a consulting room where I was examined by a doctor. In no time at all I was out of the hospital and in the bus shelter on my way back home, but Mam was crying as she had been told to go back home to pack a bag and to bring me in the following day in preparation for an operation. I put my arms around her. "Don't worry, Mam, I'll be all right."

Because there were no beds in the children's ward I was admitted to an adult ward and shortly after I was operated on to remove the mastoid bone from my inner ear.

One time I was woken up in the early hours of the morning by sounds coming from the next bed. Through a chink in the curtains I saw young redheaded woman unconscious and there seemed to be some urgency as the doctors and nurses seemed to work on her. She wasn't there when I woke up the following morning, perhaps I had dreamt it?

I must have been really quite poorly, because my dad came to see me and he was terrified of hospitals, but I really enjoyed my spell in hospital. I was a child in an adult ward so I was spoiled rotten whenever the other patients were discharged. They would leave me their drinks and goodies some of which my mother took home for Mel. He was probably at home hoping I would stay in hospital forever! When I was discharged my mother brought me a lovely pair of black velvet boots to go home in to replace my clogs. Fox Lane Junior school had made a collection for me and with it my mam had bought me the boots. I was very disappointed. I didn't want boots. All I wanted was a basket of fruit, like the ones I'd seen in the hospital.

When I arrived home an air-raid shelter had been built at the bottom of the Crescent obstructing my view of Mr. Dean's lovely garden, and while I was in hospital Mel had managed to crash into it on his bike, hurting his arm. The shelter already stank, just like Mam said it would.

When I went back to school I must have looked a sorry sight. It was no wonder that my fellow classmates avoided me, worried that 'it' might be catching. I must admit I must have looked a little strange with my hair half shaved off and a bandage over my left ear, which impaired my hearing. But even when the bandages came off I still couldn't hear too well. Unfortunately it made people think that I was a bit slow. I was all right with a one to one conversation but I could not cope with a crowd.

While the man at number 34 had been called up, he'd managed to get an army desk job, so came home a fair bit and now his wife was pregnant. Her niece Doreen from Preston had come to live with her aunt until after the baby was born. Doreen was older than me, and as she'd displayed at the cinema, a little more streetwise. She would stand no nonsense off anyone, especially the lads in the street, so she was the perfect companion to travel on the school bus with when no one else would sit next to me.

My hair was growing back, but I still had my hospital dressing on when Nurse Hughes, the dreaded nit nurse, paid a visit to the school. I was found to be infected so I was not allowed to go back into class. I was immediately taken to the cloakroom for my coat then escorted off the premises. I had no money so I couldn't catch a bus home, and it would be hours before the school bus came along. I didn't know the short cut home through the fields, so I had to follow the bus route of which I was familiar with. The school bus went down Fox Lane then at the junction at Seven Stars it turned right onto Leyland Lane to Earnshaw Bridge. Fox Lane at that time was being used as a proving ground by Leyland Motors for its tanks, and there was one currently sharing my route.

The tanks would trundle down the lane swaying from side to side churning up the road as they went. When the tank got to the junction at the bottom of Fox Lane the drivers sometimes would be unable to negotiate the turn and clip one of the houses, often causing a great deal of damage. Knowing this, it was quite frightening to be on the Lane at the same time as a tank, even keeping my distance, there was still a chance of getting hit by a piece of churned up tarmac, so I was very glad when I arrived home safely. As I had no key and was too tired to play in the fields, I sat in the lavvy until Mam came home from work in the afternoon, but at least I had Bonzo to keep me company.

The following morning Mam took me to the school clinic in Hastings Road, a doctors' surgery just for children, at the top of Golden Hill where I had this awful smelly gunk put on my head. We came away from the clinic with a steel tooth comb and a bottle of the gunk which Mam had to put on my head until the little perishers had completely gone. Still it could have been worse, the children at the clinic who had impetigo had their sores painted purple. Most of them were crying because the treatment stung their faces, and I was now off school for a few days at least.

When I went back to school the dressing from behind my ear had been removed and my hair had grown enough to be cut into a bob. My fellow classmates were none the wiser as to why I had been off school. At least I thought so.

Fox Lane Junior was a happy school. It was run by a forward thinking Headmaster who had a fondness for music. Whenever I passed the school hall there always seemed to be a girl singing about bees. I was told she was practicing to sing for the B.B.C. I never knew her and wonder if she ever made it as a singer. It was at Fox Lane where I fell in love with poetry. Once a week our teacher would read us poems by Walter de la Mare or Alfred Noyes. My favourite poem was called 'The Highwayman'. For a short while I would lose myself in an imaginary world of unrequited true love. The poem that won me my one and only merit card at school was called 'The Scarecrow'. I was so enthralled with this poem that I spent the weekend making a tiny scarecrow which I placed on my teacher's desk on Monday morning, much to her delight.

* * *

Whenever my Uncle Andy was on duty Aunt Irene would visit us. I liked my aunt, she was fun. She was a younger version of my mam. If she stayed the night she would entertain my brother and I with stories of when she used to dance and sing in the cinemas and clubs with her sister Mildred.

"We did a clog dance dressed as a little Dutch girl and boy, I was the girl and my sister was the boy. Once we did a dance as wooden soldiers, we danced mechanical fashion. That was a hard dance to do, but it helped to win us a few competitions. I once won a medal at a theatre in Preston with an English clog dance, the judge put chalk on the heels of my clogs, and then I had to dance on a small square of glass. If there had been any chalk on the glass when I finished the dance I would have been disqualified, and you had to do the right number of steps, because they were counting them.

"I had managed to get a part in a production of 'Babes in the Wood' in London, and I was just beginning to enjoy myself when my mam came down to London and took me out. I had to go back home to work, because now that my little sister was at grammar school the family needed my wages. That was the end of my show business career!"

On one occasion when Aunt Irene visited me, she asked me to paint her legs with 'Gold Mist', which were liquid stockings out of a bottle. When her legs had dried

I carefully drew a line down the back of her legs with an eyebrow pencil. I had to be exceptionally careful as one wobble and the whole operation would have to be started from scratch. She must have been pleased with the result because the next time she came to stay she asked me to do it again. The stocking shortage caused the female population to experiment with all kinds of concoctions, the favourite one being painting your legs with gravy browning. The Yanks were quick to take advantage of the shortages in order to gain favour with their girlfriends, getting hold of 'nylons' for them. In return, when bottles of cold tea were sold to the Yanks as the finest whisky, it was one big laugh.

One morning we heard the dreadful news about a jeep load of Americans going back to base after a night out being involved in a terrible accident at Pack Saddle Bridge at Euxton. The bridge was a very low one and by standing up in the jeep going under it, at least one of the soldiers had their head taken clean off with others badly injured. The blackout, and the absence of traffic lights on a bridge that was only safe for a vehicle with any height to go under it in the middle, were probably the main causes of the accident. The whole sad incident was talked about for weeks. I don't know if the deceased was taken home or if he was buried in the American War Cemetery at Madingly in Cambridgeshire.

Chapter Twenty

The arrival the Americans had caused some excitement in our part of Lancashire. But at Bamber Bridge, or 'The Brigg' as everyone from Leyland had for some reason always called it, there was an increased curiosity as some of the soldiers were black. Dorothy had ridden her bike to The Brigg just so she could see what a black man actually looked like. She reported back that she didn't see what all the fuss was about.

In Bamber Bridge, they were more than welcome. The only occasional animosity to them being, as it was with their white counterparts, was that they were three years late and our sons had been dying while they'd been eating like kings, listening to jazz in speakeasies, or whatever it was they did over there.

But the soldiers at the US Eighth Army Air Force Station 569, 1511 Quartermaster Truck regiment had brought with them age old prejudices that had no place in that small Lancashire town. You have to remember that racial segregation was still alive and well in the USA at this point in time, but the Briggers didn't see colour, they saw lads thousands of miles away from home just like their own sons. But trouble had been simmering at The Brigg for some time between the two factions of G.I.s. The trouble was no longer confined to the camp, but had started spilling over into the pubs and the shops in the area.

Having to queue had always been an unwritten law until now, but to make sure manners were upheld in a time of war and shortages, a recent bylaw had been passed which stated that *'Whenever six or more people are congregated together at bus stops or in shops they have to form an orderly queue'*. To refuse to obey this law was seen as treacherous, culprits refusing to obey this law were to be dealt with severely. The American soldiers generally obeyed this law, but they had their own segregated interpretation. Whenever they went into the local shops they would join the end of the queue and patiently wait their turn, but if there was a black soldier in the queue and a white one came along, he would have to go to the back of the queue and give the white soldier his place. This kind of behaviour incensed the local people and it wasn't long before they began to take sides.

Whilst the unit was mixed, all the officers bar one were white, as were all of the MPs[12], and those in command decided to defuse the chances of trouble in the pubs, they would demand the pub landlords should ban US soldiers on the basis of their colour, as happened back at home.

Reluctantly, because it would mean turning away good trade, the landlord at The Olde Hob agreed, just not the way the Americans had assumed he would. The next day there was a sign outside that told the white GIs they were no longer welcome.

On the 24th June 1943, tension at The Brigg boiled over into what would become known by us as the 'Battle of Bamber Bridge'. Some said it was a 'mutiny', whilst the official line at the time was that nothing whatsoever happened that night. But even back home the sound of gunfire was carried on the night air. Mam knew it

---

[12] Military Police

couldn't be Euxton as they exploded their reject ammunition during the afternoon in daylight hours, and it couldn't be German paratroopers as there had been no sound of planes that night.

* * *

It didn't take long before the news of a mutiny at Bamber Bridge came into the street. The following day rumours abounded about soldiers being shot in the back by gun happy MPs. It was said that black soldiers had broken into the armoury holding siege there in fear of their lives. That evening the Lancashire Evening Post printed a small article which denied that anyone had been hurt in the 'skirmish', but did admit it happened. The following day a communiqué by the Americans stated that only one person had been hurt. All leave at the base was cancelled and a blanket of silence was thrown over the whole unhappy affair. When Andy visited some time later, all efforts by neighbours to find out what really happened that night were met with stony silence.

What had happened was that chucking out time at the pub, had almost turned into a full-blown military conflict; an American race riot with access to serious weaponry, in the rural Lancastrian village of Bamber Bridge.

It had been a ten p.m. closing time at The Olde Hob, something the Americans, black or white had never been happy with, neither had the locals, nor the British servicemen and women who were there that night, so there were boos and jeers as there were most nights at closing time. Then two US MPs appeared, with one spotting that a single black soldier of the many who was there was 'improperly dressed', and thought it would be a good idea to try and arrest him. Then the rest of the pub, which would have included many 'improperly dressed' Brits, surrounded him and told him it simply wasn't happening. Over-reacting on top of his initial over-reaction, the MP drew his gun. A bottle may have been brandished; a bottle may have been thrown at the jeep as they retreated. It may well have been both.

As the black soldiers then walked back to base, with British ATS girls and locals on their way home in tow, the reinforced MPs tried their arrest again, and fists, bottles and cobblestones flew, to be met with bullets. The crowd dispersed, but the damage was done as one of the black soldiers was shot in the neck.

On returning to the camp, the black soldiers had gone straight to the armoury. Whilst the single black officer in the unit had tried to calm things down, the arrival of a makeshift armoured vehicle after his plea for calm changed that. More shots were fired and more people on both sides were injured, whether by bullets, bottles or cobbles. Somehow, the 'mutiny' as the US Army would come to accept it was, fizzled out and Private William Crossland was the only person, one of the black soldiers who had been shot, to die that night.

There were a couple of trials following the Battle of Bamber Bridge, with twenty year sentences for various crimes being commuted with almost everyone back on duty within a year.

Fifty years later when Andy paid us a visit, I asked him about the trouble at The Brigg, and I thought that because so many years had gone by since that night I might be told the truth about what really happened, I was shocked when he shouted, "Nothing happened! It was all lies!"

As Dad had said at the time, "While they are fighting each other they are not securing the area against attacks by the Luftwaffe. If the Germans ever score a hit on Euxton we'll all go up regardless of colour."

Private William Crossland is buried in the American War Cemetery in Cambridgeshire, plot F, row 7, grave 65.

Chapter Twenty-One

I spent the next four years at Wellfield Secondary Modern School. While boys and girls had most of their lessons together, the playgrounds were separate. Like most schools of that style, the boys' playground and bike shed was to the right, and the girls' playground and bike shed was to the left. The two playgrounds were separated by steps, at the top of which was a door which led to the Headmaster's study and staff room. Running alongside of the girls' playground was a pair of double gates which was the main entrance to the school.

At nine sharp every morning the door at the top of the steps would open and the duty teacher for that week would come out and blow two sharp blasts on their whistle. The first was a signal for everyone to stand as still as statues and on the second whistle all pupils had to form class lines. Then in a silent, disciplined and orderly fashion we would all march into the hall for the daily assembly.

This school was run by a draconian Headmaster who would stand by the duty teacher, watching for latecomers. It was woe betide anyone who was trying to sneak through the gates after the whistle.

I remember one lad called Jimmy; he was always late because of all the chores he had at home to do before coming to school. He would hide behind the gate posts at the school entrance waiting for a chance to sneak into school, but to no avail the eagle eyed Headmaster always spotted him. *"In my study, boy!"* he'd bellow, with a sinister emphasis on the 'boy'.

We girls did try to help Jimmy. We would signal to him to go back up the street to wait until the Head had gone into the hall for morning assembly, but it never worked. Jimmy was always up for the cane.

One thing everyone knew was that the Head had a penchant for the English Teacher.

The older boys who were sent for the cane soon sussed out that if they barged into the Head's study, instead of standing outside the door shaking, they would only get a ticking off from a very flustered Headmaster, who more likely than not would have the English teacher sat on his knee. I know this to be true because I was once given a message by my form teacher to take to the Head's study. I was told to knock on the door and if I didn't get an answer I was to leave it on his desk. I knocked didn't get an answer so I went in and saw the Head sat in his chair, with the English teacher sat on him, fondling each other.

The Head hated clogs as the clattering noise they made on his nice marble floors seemed to infuriate him. As far as the Head was concerned, clogs differentiated between the poor and the affluent pupils attending his school, but it seemed to me at the time that it was the clog wearers who got the cane more often than the shoe wearers.

One of the most useful lessons I had in my first year at school was needlework. I was taught how to use a sewing machine and make patterns which proved to be very useful in later years when I made my own clothes. The first term at school I made a green check apron with matching headband. This was to be my uniform for the

Domestic Science class in the second term, which like needlework was of course just for the girls. Boys did joinery and metalwork.

The first lesson of the new term was like teaching me to suck eggs, as I had to wash, starch and iron the garments I'd made the previous term, something I'd been doing with Mam for years. The second lesson wasn't teaching us to suck eggs, but actually how to boil them. Of course that wasn't as bizarre as it may now sound. Whilst boiling an egg is possibly the simplest cooking task there is, eggs were rationed to one per week, so no one would ever waste an egg by boiling it when there was baking to be done.

Afterwards we were taught how to make different types of pastries. We made fish pies, cottage pies with corned beef, cheese pies, Irish stew, and of course the Woolton vegetable pie. The Woolton pie was named after Lord Woolton head of the Ministry of Food, and found in 'Potato Pete's Recipe Book'. It was named after Woolton but because people didn't want to eat this completely vegetable pie when the recipe was first promoted by his Ministry, he would religiously eat it in front of the newspaper cameras.

We made fairy cakes, jam tarts, swiss rolls, Eve's pudding and my favourite, the Victoria sandwich cake. Just before the Christmas holidays we made a Christmas cake and mince pies. The cake was saved for home, but the mince pies got eaten there and then. The school supplied us with vegetables from the school garden, but all the other ingredients we had to bring from home, so it was important that the finished product made it back home. If we forgot our headbands we would have to wash up, clean the stove or clean out the stock room. I was cleaning out the stock room one day after a delivery of chocolate powder and jam from Australia. I kept dipping my finger in the sweet powder and as a result I broke out in an itchy rash which I couldn't hide from anyone.

When the school bell signalled the end of the lesson we would put what we had cooked into our baskets. As soon as we stepped outside the Domestic Science room there would be a crowd of hungry boys waiting to cadge anything they could. I wasn't very popular because besides the mince pies, everything I made I always took home for tea. I always thought that the boys should have had cookery lessons, and the girls should be shown how to mend fuses and read meters. We were to be the post-war generation of future wives and mothers, so the domestic propaganda had to start in the schools. But, the war had given the women folk of England a taste of independence and they liked it. No longer would they accept the lives of their mams' drudgery of the kitchen sink and the pain of endless child bearing.

According to the men, "The women had grown horns."

* * *

Now that I was at senior school it was my job to pick up the weekly groceries. The school wasn't far from our registered grocery shop, so every Friday I would take the shopping list my mother had given me. On arriving at the shop I would hand the list and the ration book over the counter and then wait patiently whilst the manager and her assistant weighed and packed our weekly rations up in the back room. My basket packed and the groceries paid for I then walked the two miles over the fields home.

Once home, my mother would unpack my bag and check everything. For the last few weeks there had always been something missing from my basket. This particular week it was cheese. Mam realised it was not a result of my carelessness, because it was simply happening too often. The recipe for the next cookery lesson was cheese pie, and because I hadn't any cheese to take to school I knew I would end up cleaning the ovens.

That Monday the new girl to the class, whose mother happened to be the new manager at our registered shop, brought into the class not the proverbial 'apple for the teacher', but a huge chunk of cheese. I couldn't help but think that my lack of cheese and her surplus of it, which wasn't even going to the cooking class but was a present for the form teacher, might be connected. On hearing this, Mam became even more motivated than she had been before to 'visit' the shop and have a word. I never 'lost' anything from that shop again.

The new girl had been given a desk at the front of the class, which I had hoped to get, because following my operation sitting at the back of the class presented me with hearing problems. It was because of my hearing I rarely put my hand up to answer questions just in case I had misheard. Eventually I became invisible.

One lesson I did enjoy was art. I always came top of the class. The marks I received for art always helped to get me a respectable end of term report. The Art teacher, Miss Docherty, was disabled in one arm but she could draw beautifully with the other one. I used to pass her coming out of her lodgings every morning. I always wanted to speak to her, but felt if I did it would look like she was favouring me at lessons. Silly really.

One Monday morning the school was filled with a dread the Luftwaffe could not have matched. The nit nurse Miss Hughes had returned. We all knew what that meant. If she found you were infected you would be sent home immediately and the shame would last all term. The only one in our class who was found to have head lice was the new girl. I knew she would have to go to the clinic with all the others that had been found to be infected. There she would have the evil smelling gunk rubbed into her head until all the nits were dead, and only be allowed back to school when she was clear.

The school was visited again, this time by a Government Department who had come to measure the feet of every pupil in the school. Those pupils who were found to be size two or over were issued with extra clothing coupons. I just qualified with size two and a half. My mam was very pleased with my big feet, as was every other parent whose child qualified for the extra coupons.

I recall school dinners with fond memories. Today, people who have never been hungry poke fun at school dinners, but my brother and I enjoyed them. Yes we did have sago, (frog spawn), semolina and rice, but we had jam roly-poly, spotted dick, queen of puddings, apple pie all with lashings of custard. We had hotpots with crust, sausage and mash, fish and chips on Fridays and my favourite 'Irish stew'. Now and again we were given apples or pears. School dinners were simply the only hot meals that many of us had. For some children at the school, it was the only meal they had.

My brother Melvin was at Fox Lane Junior School in 1946 when the eleven plus was implemented. The eleven plus exam gave bright successful children from poorer families a place in grammar schools and one day a chance to go to university, but the exam or at least the system was massively unfair. Boys did not have to achieve as high a grade to get into grammars. At Wellfield Secondary Modern the more able pupils took the thirteen plus, passing this exam meant they would have a chance to go to a College in Preston. The boys would learn a trade, become draughtsmen or eventually work in banks. The girls would train to become secretaries or take up employment at Owen and Owens, that being the elite store at the time. A thirteen year old girl called Audrey who sat next to me in class passed the exam and went to Art College at Preston. Another girl who passed the exam wasn't so lucky she was sent to work in the Mill by her parents. My future husband who was a pupil at Wellfield that year successfully gained a placement at a Technical College in Preston. The following year in 1947 the school leaving age was raised to fifteen so I had to stay on at school for another year. It was at Wellfield that my brother got into trouble with the gardening teacher, during a lesson Mel ate a cabbage leaf the teacher saw him and made him eat the whole cabbage, and needless to say my brother was quite ill. The teacher had recently been demobbed from the forces and was obviously suffering from post traumatic stress as a result of his war experiences, it was rumoured at the school that the teacher had been a prisoner of war so he was given a bit of leeway by the staff.

One day in my second year at Wellfield the Head announced that every pupil in the school had to pay half a crown for sports equipment. As my brother was at the school as well now, this would mean that my mother had to send five shillings which she could ill afford, and trying to get the money from my dad caused endless rows. It wasn't unusual for Mel to get the cane, but when I got caned, my father relented and my brother and I got the money. I remember the caning vividly. I was ordered to the front of the class and was caned on my hand along with a boy called Stanley in front of my classmates. "That will teach you not to forget," said my teacher.

The teacher's name was Mrs. Sergeant a name I have never forgot, nor have I forgot the name of my companion in disgrace, a nice lad called Stanley, who like me came from a poor family.

Chapter Twenty-Two

Turning the corner of the Crescent sometimes filled me with dread, because I never knew what to expect. Once it had been the news about little Eva, then it was my drunken Uncle Andy tearing up and down the street on my 'sit up and beg' bike shouting to all and sundry, *"I've been married for ages and there's still no sign of a baby,"* until Mam dragged him indoors telling him off for shaming his wife. Andy and Irene never did have any children of their own, so they adopted two brothers Mark and Eddie. They had adopted Mark first, but when his disabled brother Eddie had come to visit, and held on to his brother for dear life when it was time to go, their hearts had melted and they quickly adopted him too.

***

Turning into the Crescent on this particular occasion I felt uneasy especially when I saw a number of cars parked at the bottom of the street outside our house. Running down the Crescent I was met by Mrs. B who ushered me into her house. Once inside she told me that my Dad had been involved in an accident with his lorry and a double decker bus. He had been taken to hospital with head injuries but had refused to stay. Mam had asked Mrs. B to look after my brother and myself until the doctor and all the other visitors had gone. Neighbours told me afterwards my dad was lucky as the fire brigade who cut him out of the cab didn't expect to find him alive.

Dad was never the same after the accident, and his behaviour towards my brother worsened. The slightest misdemeanour on my brother's part and off would come my dad's belt and Mel would get a thrashing which was often unjustified. One day, Mel came in from playing football and for no reason at all that I could see, Dad threw a shoe at the back of his head, but Mel just laughed. I had used to wonder why some men wore braces and a belt, but now I realised the braces were so their pants wouldn't fall down, when they took off their belt and decided to administer discipline to their offspring, justified or unjustified.

Previously, Dad had bought Mam a watch from a spiv. Mam, not used to wearing a watch had put it in the dresser drawer which is where I saw it. One day I wore it for school but it didn't work so I placed it back in the drawer as soon as I got home and forgot about it. The following day my brother got a severe walloping for breaking the watch. I owned up to wearing the watch, but added that the watch was already broken. Mam said that when Dad found out the watch was broken he smashed it, put it in the bin and then blamed Mel.

I was upset because I loved my brother. I'd loved him since he was a baby when I tried to stick all his lovely golden curls back on his head after Dad had given him a haircut. I loved him when I carried him home piggy-back after he had hurt his leg on a roundabout at Earnshaw Bridge, and I didn't want him getting blamed for something he hadn't done. Living with Dad after his accident was like walking on egg shells. Even Mam was getting the brunt of his temper until one evening, even she'd had enough. After a blazing row she stormed out of the house, went over the fields, climbed through

Forester's hedge, and got stuck. Dad had to pull her out the hawthorn hedge and rescue her from the herd of curious cows that had congregated around her.

Dad never went back to work on the wagons after his accident. Instead, he got work as a fitter's mate at Stannings the Bleacher and Dyers over the fields. So it was an end to the extra sausages from the butchers, which was a blow because they were now rationed, and even if he could have afforded it, he wouldn't be able to buy petrol on the pretence it was for the car, because now you couldn't get petrol for private cars unless you were a doctor or someone important like that. But after being in his new job for a few weeks he started coming home with winceyette rags which he had been given to wipe his oily hands on. Dad and I would cut the rags into squares, and sew them together turning them into bedspreads. Dad was a good sewer, when he'd been on the dole he'd helped out by sewing some of the costumes for Spick and Span.

We had recently been given a sewing machine from my Great Aunt Elizabeth in Wigan after her cottage had been compulsory purchased to make way for a new road. The old lady had held out to the bitter end against the town planners before being forcibly moved. When the war was over, many of the returning soldiers would lose their homes to town planners in a similar way under the pretence of 'slum clearance' for ring roads, shopping centres or tower blocks, with notices saying 'no ball games' or 'keep off the grass'. However Great Aunt Elizabeth's sewing machine was a godsend and we got so good at sewing the bedspreads we even gave the bedspreads away as wedding presents to grateful friends and would swap them for rations.

Chapter Twenty-Three

One Saturday morning I woke to the most dreadful racket coming from the Bradley's back garden. Next door's geese were running around the garden trying desperately to outrun Maggie, who was chasing them. As soon as she got hold of them, she was going to strangle them, but I think the geese had figured this out. Our neighbours were shouting encouragement to the whole sorry episode. On our side, Bonzo was going berserk. Mel and I dashed downstairs to see Mam hanging on to the dog, who was on the draining board trying to get though the tiny window to save her friends, who in her mind weren't randomly honking, but shouting *"Help!"* Mam was exhausted, so my brother and I had to hang on to the dog for dear life. Despite the fact they always chased her off when she got in their pen, Bonzo regarded the geese as family. We knew if Bonzo had managed to break through the window she would have attacked Maggie as well as our Mrs. B.

The racket went on for ages, and then, there was silence. Bonzo began to howl, we all began to cry. Maggie had given up trying to strangle them and had dispatched them with an axe. Afterwards, Mrs. B gave us some goose meat but none of us could eat it, and Bonzo, who normally gobbled up anything left in front of her, took one sniff and refused to touch it. When Dad came home later that day he told Mam in no uncertain terms what he thought of our neighbour's cruelty. I was taught a lesson that day if you have anything derogative to say about anyone never say it in front of a child, because the next time I saw Mrs. B. I repeated word for word what my dad had said, though I can't remember a single word of it now. Needless to say my parents and our neighbours had a row. Soon, Mrs. B would move further up the street into a house which was empty because over the course of the war, both the mother and son who lived there had died. That caused another row because of the smelly mess that was left in the back garden for other people to clear up.

It wasn't long before a family of squatters moved in next door. The head of the household was an ex R.A.F. man and our landlord took them to court in an attempt to evict them, but the mood of the media and the people, and more importantly the court, was against him. The family won the right to stay a decision, which pleased my dad. Our new neighbours turned out to be a very nice family.

Chapter Twenty-Four

It was ages since there had been an air raid and there was a feeling that the war was turning. Things seemed different, like something was happening. There were fewer servicemen about, more trucks and trains and the gossip in the playgrounds and the street was that production at the factories had changed and increased. Even Mam, who believed completely in the wartime mantra that *'Loose lips sink ships'*, had let slip that the rubber works had been working on a pipeline that could go under the sea.

After years of being on the back foot, people wanted to believe that an invasion would happen soon. In an industrial town where almost everyone over the age of fourteen was involved in war work, everyone wanted to know that the little bit of information they had pointed to the hope that the invasion of German occupied Europe was coming, and they craved for more news to validate their prayer that the war soon might be over.

And soon that prayer was answered when on the 6th June 1944 Winston Churchill told Parliament that the invasion had begun. Prayers were said in churches and schools all over the country for the success of the invasion. Even though it was summer, every night we would now be at home listening to the latest news of the invasion on the wireless. Whilst we hoped it might be over in weeks, Dad offered his wisdom. "This won't be like how the Germans took Europe so fast, this will take longer, they will make us fight all the way to Berlin."

Of course he was right, and not long after, Aunt Irene was in our house, trying not to cry, but failing miserably. Uncle Andy had been shipped off.

* * *

Mam loved Christmas. We would begin preparing for the Christmas holidays about two weeks before Christmas Eve. My brother and I would carefully wrap apples and pears with brown paper and the fruit would be stored in the dresser drawer so that they would be nice and ripe for Christmas. Christmas trees were a black market luxury that most people couldn't afford, especially us, but a week before Christmas we would climb over the stile at the bottom of Edgehill Crescent scramble through a gap in the hedge which separated Forester and Cherry Ripes fields, and carefully avoiding the cow pats in the field we would head for a little copse in the middle of Forester's field where we would forage on the forest floor for pine cones and any interesting branches we could find.

When we found a large interesting branch we took it home then Mel and I helped Mam to paint it white, and while it was still sticky Mam would then sprinkle the branch with 'stardust' so that it sparkled. This would be our 'Christmas tree'. We spent the next few days hanging the cones from the 'tree' with ribbon and coloured wool. We made paper chains and paper angels which we dotted around the tree. Pride of place was a lovely peg fairy covered in coloured tissue paper which we placed on the topmost branch of our 'tree'.

Best of all was when Mam made the Christmas pudding; the house would be filled with the sweet smell of spices. We would all take turns in stirring the pudding making sure we made our Christmas wish. Then Mam would put the pudding mixture in muslin cloth to be steamed, but before she did she put a silver joey[13] in the pudding. Whoever got the coin on Christmas Day was the one who got the wish. A few days before Christmas Eve a bottle of sherry would take pride of place on the dresser ready for visitors. I'm afraid the sherry got watered down by my brother and me more than once.

It was the 22nd December 1944, and school had broken up for the Christmas holidays, so I went to meet Mam from work, taking a couple of bags with me because I knew she would be loaded up. As she crossed the road to meet me I could see that something was wrong. As I helped her with the parcels she began to cry. Mam had scalded her arms in the canteen where she worked, but she had stayed till the end of her shift so she could get a share of the perishable food that was left. Because Mam was so poorly with her burns, she stayed in bed all through Christmas. We didn't sing carols that Christmas, and Dad didn't play his mouth organ. Even opening our presents wasn't the same without Mam. Our wish that Christmas was for Mam to get better soon.

On Christmas Eve we were woken up by a loud bang in the early hours of the morning. Bonzo was barking and besides Mam, we all came out of our bedrooms, wondering what had happened.

"What was that, it wouldn't have been Euxton going up would it?" I asked.

---

[13] Better known as a 'Thruppenny Bit', or for those born after decimalisation, a three pence coin.

"No chance. If that was Euxton, we wouldn't be here to talk about it," replied Dad, before adding, "It couldn't have been a raid, there weren't any sirens."

"Or engines," I added.

"I thought I did hear an engine, but I might have been dreaming." was Melvin's useless contribution.

"It was probably one of ours going down nearby then," was Dad's conclusion and we debated whether or not it was worth going back to bed or not.

It turned out that what we had heard was a V1 that had been targeted at Manchester, and coming down in Bamber Bridge. It had missed by quite a way. Better than that, just like the old propaganda news story, it actually had come down on a chicken coop, cooking someone's Christmas dinner a day early.

* * *

Now, almost all the news about the war was good news, then one Saturday at the flea pit, there was the Belsen newsreel. No one who saw it remembers the film they saw that day, and whilst normally the newsreel was met with booing or cheering, this time there was just silence. It didn't seem like we were looking at people, more so skeletons with their skin still on.

If anyone was in doubt about the justness of the war, those horrific scenes of the liberation of Belsen by British troops soon put an end to that, we now knew what the war had really been about. The Belsen newsreel is in some ways like the air raids, women painting their legs, and rationing. It's a memory that everyone who lived through the war has ingrained in their memory forever. Everyone who saw it remembers the Belsen newsreel, for the first time we had seen what we had really been fighting against, not Germans, but Nazis.

No one spoke as they left the cinema, and no matter how much they wanted to, no one forgot what they saw.

* * *

On the same day as the liberation of Bergen-Belsen, 15th April 1945, the clock faces of Big Ben were lit up for the first time in six years, signifying the blackout was over. This sent a message of hope and joy the length and breadth of the country.

Chapter Twenty-Five

I was at home on 8th May 1945 when the victory bells rang out throughout the land and Prime Minister Winston Churchill announced the end of the war in Europe. The news sent people laughing and crying into the streets, and those that could headed for London, those that couldn't sat glued to their chairs listening to the radio. At ten-thirty p.m. from the Ministry of Health building in Whitehall, Winston Churchill gave a speech to the jubilant crowds below and this is the gist of some of it.

"My dear friends, this is your victory. This is not the victory of a party or any class or any spare land section of the community. It is a victory of the great British nation as a whole; we were the first in this ancient island to draw the sword against tyranny. We were left alone for a whole year; did anyone want to give in? Were we down hearted?"

"No," the crowd roared.

He ended his speech with the words, "This is your victory, God bless you all!"

But many in the crowd replied that he was wrong, and this was *his* victory.

The crowd then sang 'Land of Hope and Glory' with such gusto I'm sure it must have been heard all the way to Berlin.

We had initially rushed out into the Crescent to hug everyone we saw, and now celebrations were in full swing. All our neighbours in the Crescent rejoiced together all laughing, singing and dancing. People who couldn't stand the sight of each other days before were now hugging and kissing each other. A piano had been rolled from the top of the street to the air-raid shelter, which had now become a stage. Dad got up on to the shelter and played his mouth organ to the happy crowd below. A neighbour sang along with him, impersonating Vera Lynn. Dixie Dean did a tap dance, someone played a piano accordion and everyone danced. Mrs. B did the Can-Can on the shelter showing her huge posterior covered in a pair of Union Jack knickers. Had she somehow just made them, or had she stolen a flag years ago and been wearing them for years? Who cared!

The identity of the mystery piper who'd been the bane of the air raid wardens, who he'd always managed to evade every year as he'd gone out in the field to pipe in the New Year was now revealed, as he walked up and down the street in full regalia blowing his bagpipes.

Cakes, trifles, tinned fruit and cream as well as tinned salmon appeared from nowhere. It seems everyone in the street had been hoarding goodies for months in anticipation for the end of the war. The neighbours all worked together and decided that at the end of the week we would all celebrate again by having a street party.

As it turned out we had another reason to celebrate that weekend. Word had come through from Chorley that my Aunt Louie had just had a baby boy. Aunt Louie and Uncle Phillip called their new baby 'Victor'

Embarrassed at the antics of the grown-ups I went to a huge bonfire which was blazing away on the corner of Earnshaw Drive. A transport firm on Golden Hill had contributed some old tyres so the fire kept blazing until the early hours of the morning. Then, tired but happy people began to drift home, happy in the knowledge that they would be safe in their beds from now on. Our street was lit up from top to bottom as most of the neighbours had ripped down their hated blackout curtains. To my eyes at that time it looked like fairyland, but I was half expecting the warden to come tearing down the street on his bike blowing his whistle and shouting, *"Put that bloody light out,"* at the sailor who was sending Morse code to his girlfriend across the street, telling her it was safe to come over as his mam had gone to bed.

The next few days I helped Dad machine red, white and blue bunting which we strung over the bottom end of the street from neighbour to neighbour. I made a large red rose with the spare material. This we placed on the arch over the front door. One of our Irish neighbours asked, "What's that?"

"It's the red rose of Lancashire," I said proudly.

The material had come from Stannings Bleachers and Dyers over the fields, and this was the only time the material had come out of Dad's works legitimately. The Crescent was surprised to get anything at all because just recently the streets had been trawled by the factory manager looking for stolen material. A neighbour who worked at the factory had stolen part of a valuable export order and had turned the material into curtains which the manager easily identified as he looked through the windows.

At school the following week our Headmaster announced that the school was to take part in celebrations to mark the end of the war. All the schools in the area were to take part in a mass choir on the Mayfield in Leyland. Mayfield was a piece of land given by a wealthy spinster of the Parish to the people of Leyland for recreational purposes. The Headmaster went on to inform us all that the boys had to wear dark trousers, black shoes and white shirts. The girls had to wear white dresses socks and pumps. For the next few weeks non-academic lessons were cancelled whilst we practiced singing all the national anthems of all our war allies. Meanwhile Dad brought home from work pieces of white organdie that Mam and Mrs. B, the geese incident long forgotten, cobbled into a lovely dress. Mam was no sewer but on this she worked miracles, sewing each piece by hand. Mrs. B. put my hair in ringlets then produced a purple ribbon to put around my waist. Nearly all my classmates admired my dress which made me immensely proud of the effort Mam had put into making the dress. It was a lovely sunny day for the event, which went perfectly, and even our grumpy Headmaster praised us all at the following day's assembly.

Despite the wishes of the benefactor, when she died the Church sold the Mayfield to developers for houses, a pattern that was about to engulf Leyland.

Three months later, Japan surrendered after the Americans dropped atomic bombs on Hiroshima and Nagasaki. Although we were glad that the war with Japan had ended, there were no parties to mark the end of the 'forgotten war'.

* * *

When the lights finally came on in the Crescent in the winter that year it was magical. The lamppost acted as a magnet for the youth of the Crescent. That winter we would congregate under it and talk into the night about our future hopes and dreams. We didn't want a lot from life; most of the lads wanted a trade when they left school and maybe a car. Dorothy wanted to be a Butlins' Redcoat. I wanted to travel, a dream I thought at the time would be impossible. Mel, who had joined us, wanted to be a boxer. We all agreed that one day we would eventually move from the Crescent. Under the lamppost I discovered the light attracted all manner of flying insects. I freaked out when one of the little perishers hitchhiked a lift home in my hair. Mel joined an Amateur boxing club at Bamber Bridge where he went training each week with a mate from the top of the street. Whenever there was a boxing bout on at the club Dorothy and I would cycle over to the Brigg and spend the evening cheering our favourite boxers. Years later Mel went to Ireland to a boxing tournament where he won two fights in one night. He knocked his first opponent out with the opening punch, so the promoters gave him another opponent to fight later on in the evening. Mel knocked him out as well; his prize was a medal and eight pounds which he used to buy mam a ring. Looking back I suppose taking up boxing was sending a message out to dad which simply said 'Don't mess with me.' Dad was proud of Mel; he took his medal to work to show his workmates and was very upset when the medal disappeared from his locker. Mel was called up soon afterwards to do his National service and that was the end of his boxing career.

The end of the war saw many returns up and down the Crescent. Whilst the Bradley's son had survived the war, he had been deafened by the guns on his ship and chose not to move back in with his parents. The man who had left Dad his car for safe keeping was very pleased that he had done just that. Most important to me was that Maurice and Dennis were now old enough to leave the orphanage. Maurice became an apprentice at the Motor works whilst his brother Dennis got a job on a farm. As an apprentice Maurice had very little money so he couldn't go out with the lads in the Crescent at weekends, but I do remember when a crowd of us from the bottom of the Crescent coppered up[14] and went to Preston to a New Year's dance over Burton's shop. There was nothing romantic about it, we were all just mates. After that one night Maurice spent most of his time with the Preston Harriers Athletics Club, with whom he won a lot of prizes. When it came time for him to do his National Service my parents offered to look after his prizes, but he declined and sadly when he came back most of them had gone.

Many years later I met Maurice again; he thanked me for the advice my father had given. He said that his time at the Harris Orphanage had been strict but fair. As one of the older children it had been his job to comfort the younger ones when they arrived at the orphanage. He had to make their beds, polish their shoes and generally help with their well-being. He eventually got married and moved to the other side of town and I am sure Little Eva would have been proud.

---

[14] 'Coppered up' – Shared our resources.

Chapter Twenty-Six

With Andy gone and hopefully now on his way back to the USA, Aunt Irene spent a great deal of time with us, often staying for days. One night just before I went to sleep I asked her a question that I had wanted to get an answer on for years, "Aunty Irene, who was Kelly?"

"Oh." She looked at me hesitant as if making her mind up as whether to say anything at all after what seemed an age then replied, "I don't suppose it matters now that the war is over, but Joseph Kelly was a bricklayer who worked on building Euxton Munitions Factory just before I started working there. One day a site office near where he worked was broken into and a very important plan of the factory was stolen. Suspicion fell on Kelly, because shortly after the plans went missing, so did he. He got a passport, then on the pretext of going to see a friend of his, he travelled to Holland where he met up with a woman and then went on to Germany, where he stayed a short while before coming back to England.

"When he arrived back in Lancashire a few days later the police were waiting to arrest him and he was taken to Bolton Police Station, but when he was getting out of the police car, a very alert policeman saw him spit a chewed up piece of paper on the pavement. The policeman picked it up and saw it was the address of a contact in Holland. He also had £30 on him which as you know is a lot of money to be carrying around. I think he had gone to pay a large amount of money in £20 notes into a bank in London when he'd got back. Having a lot of twenties made the bank very suspicious, so they got in contact with the Lancashire Police who had of course been looking for him, so I think that's why they knew he was on his way home and they were waiting for him.

"I'm not sure about that last bit, but anyway your dad knows all about it, I'm just repeating what he said. Back when your dad was on the dole, he spent a lot of his time at the court listening to the cases, it was a bit like going to the cinema, maybe not as good, and you've got to keep quiet, but it's free to watch so it gave your dad something to do. Your dad used to tell us stories about the trials, and always did an impression of the way one of the judges said 'Hard Labour' when he gave out sentences. But I can tell you this for certain, when the case was first heard it was held at Chorley, but then they realised they had to move to the Assizes in Manchester and hold the rest of the trial in camera."

"What does held 'in camera' mean?" I queried.

"That's when they hold it in secret, so your dad couldn't go from then on, not that he'd have been able to afford to get to Manchester every day anyway. Euxton was top secret and the Government didn't want the public to know what was going on, and they would probably have to talk about lots of things that were secret to be able to give Kelly a fair trial. The magistrate said at Kelly's hearing in Chorley that a well-placed bomb by the German air force would cause a great deal of damage to the factory and a lot of casualties in the area, so I suppose the longer it had gone on in public, the more people would have worried."

"What happened to him after that, did he get hung like Lord Haw-Haw?" I asked.

"No, this was before war was declared, but he did go to prison. I think he got about twenty years."

"Hard labour?" I said slowly, trying to do the impression of the judge.

"Probably!"

"It all sounds a bit like 'The Thirty-Nine Steps'" I said, before adding, "He wasn't thinking about his family was he? I mean they would get bombed just like the rest of us wouldn't they?"

"I don't think he was thinking of his family," replied Irene. "It would have been the money. Maybe other reasons. Anyway lights out."

* * *

The thing was, what Kelly had stolen was an architect's drawing. It would have made it clear that Euxton was a massive munitions factory and a prime target for the Luftwaffe, but it wasn't a map, and besides a single lookout tower which would be next to impossible to spot from high altitude, there was no real evidence it was there. There's even a chance that after what Kelly had told the Germans, the plans were changed.

I often wondered if the German from Lostock Hall had been trained as a pilot because he was the only person who would have able to find Euxton. Anyone would have been able to make out the other factories, but finding Euxton would need local knowledge. Maybe he had been sent to work here by the German Government before the war in the first place. After all he was a premium, and someone had had to pay for that.

One day Melvin somehow came into the possession of a German prisoner of war pay book. Inside the pages the prisoner had drawn a map, showing the area and the exact the location of the R.O.F. Munitions Factory at Euxton and the Leyland Tank works. We have to be thankful that this prisoner did not escape.

* * *

Many years later, I paid a visit to the R.O.F. factory just before it was completely razed to the ground. I took photographs of part of the nine mile perimeter fence, with its rusty notice warning that 'Photography was prohibited'. The lookout tower was still standing sentinel over a long abandoned Army dugout. Giant broken pipes, which must have been part of the camouflage system, littered the area, still dripping with water. I would have taken more photos but rusty evil looking iron fences prevented me from getting any closer.

A village called Buckshaw now stands on the site. Many of the road names at Buckshaw are reminders of the past. There is a Barnes Wallis Way and an Ordnance Way. Even the pub is called 'War Horse' after a brave First World War horse. A few miles away, set in a beautiful wooded area, lays Astley Hall where a museum has been dedicated to the souls who lost their lives in both conflicts. It is a museum worth visiting for anyone interested in the world wars.

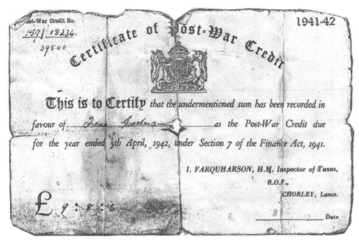

"How to Help the War"

Post War Credit was a taken out of my Aunt's wages after her weekly income tax had been deducted. It was a temporary loan to help pay for the war. Post War Credits were to be paid back after the war 'or as soon as maybe'. It took twenty-five years for the Government to honour that promise.

My mam wrote to her sisters in America to tell them of the pay-out. Only Irene wrote back, saying they were worthless to her, but perhaps mam would like to keep one as a souvenir. How much money does the government still hold in P.W.Cs never paid out?

I wonder.

Chapter Twenty-Seven

It was one of those 'good to be alive' days. The sun was shining and the smell of new mown hay wafted in on a gentle breeze from the surrounding fields. I was in the back garden pegging out the weeks washing when my task was interrupted by someone calling my name. I looked in the direction of the voice and saw a young man leaning on our fence at the bottom of the garden. I had no idea how he knew who I was and in broken English he politely asked, "Mavis, have you any cigarettes?"

I looked at him for a second, smiled then ran into the house. In the front room I opened a drawer in Mam's dresser and took out a pack of 'coffin nails'. I ran back out of the house into the garden where I handed the cigarettes to the young man. He thanked me politely then went back to a gang of men working in the field at the bottom of Broadfield Drive; I turned back to my task of pegging out the clothes. The cigarettes I had given to the young man were ones I had bought with money I had saved up. I had queued up for nearly an hour at Polly Woods's cabin on School Lane to buy the cigarettes[15].

I was going to surprise Dad when he came home for the weekend, however during the week my Aunt Irene had brought Dad two packets of twenty Camel cigarettes. I reasoned Dad would be better off with the Camel than the Woodbines or 'coffin nails' as we called them,

---

[15] The minimum age for buying cigarettes in 1945 was 16. I was 12, but had simply told the shopkeeper they were for my dad.

because each time he smoked a Woodbine he spent the morning coughing his guts up.

The same way the gun at the back of our house had appeared like a mushroom in the night, it had now disappeared overnight like a mushroom. The young man I had given the cigarettes to, belonged to a gang of P.O.W.s who were building foundations of a road, an extension of Broadfield Drive, through Cherry Ripes meadow. The road would eventually stretch to the Bleachers and Dyers half a mile away and would help to form part of a huge estate. Every morning the prisoners were marched under armed guard from their camp on the estate to work on the road.

The war had ended, but it was to be another three years before the last of the P.O.W.s were repatriated with their loved ones, and some stayed to make their homes in England, marrying local girls. Many stayed because their homes were now in East Germany which was now occupied by the Russians in a partitioned Germany. Of course it wasn't just Germans who stayed because of that. Citizens of many other countries, most notably the Poles as it had been the original invasion of Poland that brought Britain into the war, who had fought side by side with us during the war for the liberation of their homes, would have to accept that England would be their home now. During the war, the Russians had gone from being *"Those Bolshevik Bastards"* to *"Our Communist Friends"* when the German invasion of Russia had forced them to change sides, but now it was the USSR who occupied vast swathes of Europe, and had also used the war to install communist Governments, hanging their 'Iron Curtain' across the continent.

The P.O.W. camp was a magnet for the children of the area, who would go to the camp perimeter fences to throw stones and shout abuse through the wire. My brother and I kept well away. Had we gone anywhere near the camp we would probably have got walloped. One morning after my brief meeting with the prisoner, who wasn't much older than me, I found two parcels at the bottom of the garden. Inside one was a wooden duck which quacked and flapped its wings when pulled with a string; the other parcel contained a lovingly carved grey wooden heart with red roses artistically painted down each side. My brother gave his duck to our next door neighbour for her little boy. I kept my present until I gave it some years later to a German woman my mam had befriended who was having a rough time.

Prisoners of War who had been held in Canada and the USA were sent to rebuild Brain and to meet the manpower shortage left by the war, as it turned out it would be years before many of our conscripts came home, and years before the P.O.W.s also returned home.

When the prisoners in Leyland had finished working on the new Broadfield Estate they became involved in the construction of Leyland Motors Social Club in the centre of town. German P.O.W.s even had a hand in the building of Wembley Way in time for the 1948 Olympics.

Now P.O.W.s had gone contractors took over the building of Broadfield Estate. Sadly the fields that once contributed to the country's bread basket became a jungle of roads. Bannister Brook was covered over with concrete. The only indication that there had ever been a brook there at all was a road sign that simply said Bannister Drive. The brook which we had swum in, fallen in, caught tadpoles in and played war games over was now lost. Never again would we smell the sweet scent of the hawthorn hedges in the springtime when we walked along the well-trodden path down to the little nook. No longer would we hear the birds singing as they welcomed each new day, or see the haze of pink mayflowers over the meadow as we sat making daisy chains for our hair in the spring. Never again would we be able to walk along the hedges in the school holidays picking blackberries to take home for our mams to make pies with. All that was gone forever. It was one of the many sacrifices we had to make to ease the country's housing shortage caused by the war.

At the top of the Broadfield Estate the contractors hit a patch of soft sand. A hydraulic hammer was brought in to deal with the problem and for weeks steel girders were pounded into the ground night and day until people began to feel quite ill. Then one night a workman was crushed beneath the hammer so the work ceased for a short time. It was a blessed relief when the job was finished. The key to the first house was not given to a returning soldier, but to a gang foreman working on site, which didn't go down very well with the people in the Crescent.

Now the Americans had left, Washington Hall became a rehabilitation centre for men returning from Japanese Prisoner of War Camps, and the family of a similar survivor of the 'forgotten war' moved into the other half of the first semi that was built. I used to see him with his shoulders bent down like an old man as he shuffled past in his plimsolls, unable to wear shoes because the Japanese had wired his feet together to stop him from escaping. Every time he shuffled past our house, Dad would shake his head sadly, saying, "That young man is a hero."

Dad would play Colonel Bogey on his mouth organ just to annoy the German woman who Mam had found lodgings for at number 34, but she took no offence. She was a survivor. She had trekked through Germany with her sister to the safety of the British lines just hours in front of the Russian advance on the insistence of her father, an officer in the German Army. She could speak English and French fluently as well as a smattering of other languages so she was obviously an educated lady.

She married a local lad and moved to a new house on the estate. I caught up with her years later, when she came to the house just as I was administering first aid to my husband who had collapsed with a fit. Her words chilled me as she said, "If you had lived under Hitler you never would have seen your husband again."

The long talks I had with her enlightened me about life under Hitler. She said handicapped children disappeared overnight, old people dyed their hair in order to look young, and all were afraid to go into hospital for fear they may never come out. Propaganda films were made normalising euthanasia. I once saw one of those films at college; it was of a smiling husband with two young children around the bed of their equally smiling young mother who I presume had cancer. The dulcet tones of the narrator was coercing the young mother that it was her duty to accept euthanasia, 'So her family could live again'.

Had propaganda films like the one I saw made it easy for the population to turn their backs on the terrible events that had followed? I wonder.

Chapter Twenty-Eight

It was another cold day in February 1946 and my Aunt Irene was staying with us prior to leaving for America. As I was getting dressed for school I was shivering I'd put on my white blouse and brown gymslip, but I didn't have a blazer or the luxury of a cardigan to keep me warm during the day, as it would still be years before clothes rationing, any rationing, ended. My aunt promised me that when she got to America she would send me a nice warm cardigan as soon as possible.

My Aunt Irene sailed from Southampton on the Queen Mary on 23rd February 1946.

My Aunt Mildred and my new cousin Phillip had already sailed on 26th January on the luxury ship 'Argentina'. All told, eighty-thousand British women sailed for America as war brides. My aunt Mildred said years later the Argentina was a lovely ship, but I would rather have sailed on the Queen Mary! Mildred arrived in Chattanooga on 6th February where she was met by her husband's family. This is my Aunt Mildred's account of her journey which was sent to me many years after she left for America.

'Leaving England and my family was one of the most traumatic experiences of my life, but also one of the most exciting. I was twenty-three years old with an eleven month old son and a husband who was back in America waiting for us.

My whole family came to see us off. It was a tearful time for them, and a great loss. I was the youngest of eight children. We were taken to the South of England to be processed for the trip to America. We were to sail from Southampton on the privately owned luxury ship Argentina which was the first government sponsored ship for war brides. We were at the emigration centre for three days, getting our injections and having our passports checked, talking to chaplains who prepared us for our places on the ship. The Americans were well organised, but we weren't. We had British passports; our children had already been issued with American ones. The lady who shared a cabin with me was an RAF widow who married an officer in the US Air Force was travelling with four-year-old twins and pregnant with her husband's child. We were labelled, stamped, processed and ready to go.

SEEING THE WHITE CLIFFS OF DOVER FOR THE LAST TIME

26th January 1946

About five hundred brides and children sailed from Southampton on the Argentina. There were very few lights in the harbour, Britain had not recovered from six years of war and so much deprivation. The ship itself was an experience, learning how to navigate the aisles while it was rolling. There was so much food; we had gone hungry for so long it was too much at first, but by the second day those who were not seasick were ready at every meal. The children, many of them had not seen oranges or bananas were trying to eat them with the skins on. In order to give us an idea of where we would be living, we were shown travelogues of the United States. Tennessee was shown after California; what a rude awakening that was! California was shown in colour with its palm trees, the Napa Valley with its redwoods, and the glittering Pacific coast.

For Tennessee showed old black and white photos as part of a 'before and after' the Tennessee Valley Authority, which was formed in the depression to develop the area. The 'before' part of the film showed the hills of Tennessee and little shacks with wide eyed ragged children, their obvious poverty showing. Then the music, the lights and the colour changed, showing how the TVA had changed the valley into a fertile and green place. All I had been told about Tennessee children being barefoot and using out-houses seemed to have changed. This gave me some hope of a civilised place. There were just three of us coming to Chattanooga and we kept in touch for quite a long time after we got settled.

The trip to America took six days, The Atlantic was very rough. Many days we were not allowed on deck. We were kept occupied with lectures on how we were to be processed when we reached New York. Trying to get round the ship with an eleven month old child kept me occupied. Following the daily schedule we were given kept us alert and didn't leave much time to be homesick. Although at night in your cabin you wondered 'what have I done?' during the day with the entire clamour around us we felt secure.

We were taught about money exchanges and a little about the language and customs of most Americans. We were given our landing instructions: Have papers, passports etc. in hand when we land and go through customs in New York. We came into New York harbour about three a.m. in the morning, and it was a surprise to see the lights, the skyscrapers, and especially the Statue of Liberty. It was like a dream! The music on the ship was playing the American national anthem and then 'God Save the Queen'; most of us were crying with so much emotion at the sight of our new land. The Statue of Liberty stands in my memory as a symbol of a wonderful welcoming country.

The Government told our husbands not to meet us in New York, but we would be delivered to our home towns safely. Of course the New Yorkers came to get their families and were the first to disembark. We were given different colours with our name tags and were called accordingly. We were going south to Tennessee, Alabama and Georgia. The Red Cross ladies were on the docks to watch our children while we went through customs. The authorities made it very easy for us. The newspaper people were there to interview us and take pictures.

We waited in New York for an hour or so then we were transported to Penn Station by taxi, and for the first time we heard the unmistakeable Brooklyn accent. When we arrived at Penn Station there were sailors who escorted us, carrying our bags, and nappies. We were really here in America and I was on my way to Chattanooga, on the choo-choo! The train was a Pullman. It was huge in comparison with the British trains and so elegant. Lying in the bunk that night I pulled up the shade and saw miles and miles of countryside with huge red barns. Then I heard the lonesome sound of a train whistle. Our first morning on the train, we were up for breakfast only then realising that the English and American language was different. I tried to order porridge, but I had some trouble getting the waiter to understand, then an Army nurse from Alabama came over to our table and explained to him. She was coming home from England and she stayed with us until we arrived in Chattanooga. I thought if everyone in America was as kind as this young woman, I was going to be all right. The train stopped in West Virginia. A lady sat beside my son and me. She asked if she could hold him, and she remarked that he was a 'wick un' and asked where I was from. I told her England and she said, "You talk good for a furriner." I thought this was funny.

When we reached Chattanooga, we were in the last coach when I saw this man running down the platform. I realised it was my husband. It was the first time I had seen him out of uniform. His brother-in-law was there too, since he was my sponsor he was responsible for me until my husband took over. The newspaper people were there and took photos of me and my son and the other war bride, Mrs. Wilson.

My first impression of America was how 'big' everything was and how warm it was. It was the 6th February 1946 and it was as warm as a summer day back home. I have to say we looked very strange, even without our labels on our coats, but with tweeds and brogans. We looked as though we had fallen out of an Agatha Christie novel. My first meal at my brother-in-law's was so rich I couldn't eat a quarter of it.

Now adjusting to this new environment I had ship lag. I could hardly stay awake and couldn't understand why I was so sleepy. I walked to the grocery store and when I got there I was amazed at how much food there was. I looked at the produce, some of which was unfamiliar. I asked the clerk, "What was this and what was that?" He called the manager and she recognised me from my picture in the newspaper. She took me around the store filling me in on everything from the unusual things to bread. It seemed wonderland after four years of living on the edge of starvation. I went to the grocery store every day that first week until my brother-in-law said, "STOP! The war is over, and we are running out of room in the basement."

Every day was a new learning experience. I learned that even though Americans and the British spoke the same language, they were really different. The money was a challenge changing from pounds, shillings and pence to dollars and cents, but I found American money easier to handle. The temperature was and still is a problem for me. I came from a very cool part of England to the south and had a very hard time adjusting to the heat.

Also everything was so much bigger: the birds, the flowers, and even the insects. I had many funny experiences the first few months, but family, friends and neighbours helped me through it. The neighbours from where my children grew up and went to school are still some of my best friends. It was a safe and wonderful family neighbourhood where we didn't lock our doors and we could be out late at night without fear. I was accepted into the neighbourhood. I became a citizen in 1952. I spent one year in Nashville with my husband's stepmother until we could find a place of our own in Chattanooga. Then we settled in St. Elmo.

After I arrived in Chattanooga I wrote to my parents and sent them a clipping from the newspaper, remarking that "I felt right at home because it was raining."

My mother was offended and said, "If you can't say anything good about your country, don't say anything." I thought that was funny. My problems with the culture, customs and language landed me in many embarrassing situations. I had a lot to learn.

The Statue of Liberty, New York

The arrival of the first war bride ship was given a maritime welcome in New York Harbour. The arrival was flashed on cinema screens throughout the United States.

It was twenty-five years after the war before the Government honoured the promise it had made on Post-War Credits. My mam wrote to her sisters in America to tell them of the payout. Aunt Irene wrote back, saying they were now worthless to her, but perhaps Mam would like to keep one as a souvenir. I wonder just how much money does the Government still hold in Post-War Credits that was never paid out.

Chapter Twenty-Nine

It was the last needlework lesson before the breakup of the summer holidays. In two weeks' time my brother and I would be going to summer camp in Yorkshire. I was just about to sew the buttons on a pair of pyjamas when the last bell of the year went. The needlework teacher called out, "Anyone who hasn't finished their garments please put them in the cupboard until the start of next term."

I stuffed my pyjamas into my satchel and bolted for the door. I felt guilty, but my mother was waiting for them to pack into our cases. I was to have the top and my brother had the bottoms. It was a good job they were blue, he would have got ribbed had they been pink. Mam had been paying to the school holiday club for months. The price of the holiday was £5 each plus a few shillings spending money. Mrs. B had lent us a couple of suitcases and my Aunt Irene had kept her promise and had sent us a parcel from America which contained blouses, a brown cardigan, a suit for Mam, and best of all a pair of white shorts for me. There were shirts for my dad and brother, and comics. After reading and re-reading the comics I had taken them to Chorley market and sold them, splitting the money with my brother so we had extra spending money. The parcel had just come in time for our holiday!

All that week we had excitedly been packing our suitcases, then on Saturday morning, carrying our suitcases we walked across what was left of the fields with Mam and Mrs. B to school. In the school playground we were split into two groups. The boys got on one coach and the girls got on another. After a teary farewell we all waved to our parents, but by the time we had gone a few miles we were all singing. We were going to have a week without our parents and they were going to have a week of peace and quiet without us.

When we arrived at our destination, tired and hungry, sometime in the late afternoon, we were ushered into two separate wooden huts; one for the boys, one for the girls. Once inside we were lined up by two rows of beds, then after a pep talk from our teacher we emptied the contents of our suitcases into lockers. Another girl called Mavis who I had travelled up with took the next bed to me and as the week progressed we became friends. Two other schools came into camp that day, one from St. Helens and another from somewhere in the South. Meal times were always noisy, chaotic but great fun.

After breakfast the following day our school was taken to a lovely little church. As I walked into the church the lovely scent of Lily of the Valley wafted over me; even today when I smell Lily of the Valley perfume I remember that little church. During the service one of our party, a boy called Brian Gates, sang 'Oh for the Wings of a Dove'. He sang like an angel, it was beautiful. It was one of the few church services I have ever enjoyed.

The rest of the week we were taken on trips to sites of historic importance, but one day we were taken on a trip to the seaside where we were given the opportunity to have a sail around the coast, but I stayed on the beach which didn't have a hint of barbed wire. I spent my time looking for interesting pebbles to take home to my mam. When the boat sailed back to shore a number of my fellow pupils had been seasick so I was glad I had chosen to stay with my feet firmly on land.

In the evening our time was our own. Mavis and I had made friends with a couple of lads from the St. Helens school I don't remember the name of my friend's companion but mine was a redheaded lad called Peter. After the evening meal they would wait for us outside the mess hall then the four of us spent our time walking around the camp exploring the area and talking about the future. Peter wanted to be a painter and decorator just like his dad and maybe one day own his own firm. Mavis' companion was going to be a car mechanic. I hope both of them achieved their ambitions.

As the week progressed we strolled along the cliff path down to the village where we stood at the breakwater silently looking out to sea at the fishing boats. The village was a quaint huddle of stone cottages from a bygone age. Now and again a lady in a quaint bonnet would smile at us as she walked past. It was a lovely village but it had an air of sadness about it, perhaps it was an echo from the past. After so much austerity over the past few years the village shop was like an Aladdin's cave where we spent ages just browsing. On the last evening of our holidays the four of us together with my brother went into the now packed shop to spend what we had left of our money on presents for our parents.

On reaching camp that night we went our separate ways to finish our packing and put our presents away. After the evening meal our teachers told us we all had to go straight back to our huts; once inside every one of us had to empty our suitcases and put the presents that we had bought on the bed for inspection. After inspecting every bed our teacher told us to repack and put everything away. I dashed around to my brother's hut and found that they had also been told to empty their suitcases and put their presents on the bed. They too had been given the all clear. "What was it all about?" we all wondered.

After breakfast on the last day we met up with our friends from St. Helens who told us that cigarettes had been stolen from the village shop. The culprits had been caught; they were lads from the 'southern school'. After I said goodbye, Peter gave me a little pendant and my first kiss, then waving goodbye to him from the bus we both promised we would write to each other. It was a lovely holiday despite the inclement weather; it was a holiday with nice memories that will stay dear to my heart.

I didn't attend my last day at school as I didn't want to be up on the stage with my Headmaster and his mistress. I did learn years later that after many years of fooling around in his office, they did indeed get married.

After I left school, I went to work as a bookbinder at a printing works.

Chapter Thirty

As I put on my Macintosh Mam sighed. "You're not going out in this weather are you?"

It was a bitterly cold night and the rain was coming down in torrents, but I had promised my friend Barbara that I would meet her outside the Regent Cinema in Hough Lane. I really didn't want to go as I hadn't money for the bus fare into town so I would have to walk. I also knew my friend would wait for me no matter how late I was as she didn't like going into the cinema alone. I decided I would take a short cut through the unlit half built Broadfield estate instead of going the longer but safer route up Golden Hill. Stumbling my way through the darkness I eventually arrived at School Lane. I passed a Ford car on the corner and was just about to pass the British Legion when a cyclist rode past me, head down into the wind. Above the wind I thought I heard a noise. I stopped and listened but heard nothing, but a feeling of unease came over me so I walked back.

At first I could see nothing but as my eyes got accustomed to the darkness, helped by a faint light from a lamppost, I saw the cyclist laying in the middle of the road the wheels of his bike still spinning. I knew I had to get him off the road as it was a bus route. The urgency to move him grew as I heard a bus revving up in the bus depot at the top of the hill, the brakes on local buses at the time did not have a great reputation. I tried shouting but the wind carried my voice away. He was a fully grown man, I was a fifteen-year-old girl, so there was no way I would be able to move him, so I ran over to his bike which had a dynamo, stood it upside down on its saddle and handlebars in front of the unconscious man, and peddled like mad with my hands.

The light from the dynamo shone like a beacon to the oncoming bus. The bus screeched to a halt just feet away and a very angry bus conductor jumped off the bus and began cursing me for my stupidity, but he stopped his tirade when he saw the unconscious figure in the road. The screech of the bus's brakes opened doors as residents came out to investigate the noise.

"He's one of those tearabouts from Edgehill Crescent, they all have red bikes," observed one resident.

"No he isn't, and all the lads from Edgehill have blue bikes," I muttered indignantly.

An ambulance was sent for and the adults took over so I made good my escape. I ran up the hill to meet my friend who was very cross at my lateness. At work two days later I was sent for by the manager.

"What have you been doing?" asked my workmates, "There's a policeman in the manager's office asking for you."

I was terrified. Indeed, what had I done? It was of course about the accident. After asking me a number of routine questions he then asked, "Why did you turn back?"

"I heard a noise."

"What on a night like that?" he said shaking his head in disbelief. "How did you manage to see him in the dark?"

"The street light was shining on him," I replied.

"I have been doing that beat for years and I have never seen a light."

I could feel myself blushing. I was going to point out that perhaps now that the war was over the street light had been turned on, but I didn't, I kept quiet.

"Why did you stand in front of him?"

"He would have got squashed."

"You both might have got killed."

"No I don't think so," and with that the interview was at an end, but that wasn't the last I saw of the policeman. When he turned up at my house a few days later, I was very embarrassed. Normally, the only time the police came into Edgehill Crescent was to arrest someone. The curtain twitchers had a field day, and I hadn't told my mam and dad about what had happened. All I wanted to do was forget about the whole thing, but I ended up getting a commendation from the police and sometime later I found out the man was a farmer's son by the name of Mortimer. I hope he recovered, but I never did find out.

Chapter Thirty-One

Not long after my aunts left for a new life in America there was another flu epidemic. Granddad became ill and died of double pneumonia exacerbated by his emphysema.

Grandma was alone for a while, then one day her well-meaning son Phillip arrived at her house with some potential lodgers, a family of D.P.s who were about to be turned out of their accommodation in Chorley. D.P.s, or to give them their proper name, 'Displaced People' were the casualties of war who couldn't go back to the country of their birth for one reason or another, who today would be called refugees. They were people without papers, people with no identities, people without a country.

It was rumoured amongst the locals in this area that some of the D.P.s were not the victims of Hitler's Germany, but guards who had worked at the notorious concentration camps. Nevertheless, the big hearted British people welcomed them into the country. A number of D.P.s came into Lancashire to the M.O.D. hostels, which had previously housed the war workers during the hostilities.

At the first opportunity I cycled the eight miles over to my grandma's house to have a look at her lodgers. My first impression of them was one of curiosity. The parents and daughter were small and dark whereas the son was a tall blonde blue eyed boy who introduced himself in excellent English as John. His sister was around the age of my brother and John was about my age. I had hoped that whenever my brother and I visited my grandma during the school holidays the four of us would get on our bikes and explore the countryside, but no, whenever John spoke to me in English his sullen sister would intervene. Only once was he ever able to talk to me and that was when he was mending a puncture on his dad's bike in the back garden. He told me that his father was not his father and... before he got any further he was interrupted this time by his 'dad'. I have always wondered what else he was about to tell me.

One Monday morning the rent collector, who happened to be a friend of my grandma's took her to one side and told her that her lodgers, accompanied by a priest, had been to the town hall and put in a claim for her house. Because there were four of them and only one of her, they made the case to the council that they needed it more. I would be putting it mildly if I said my grandma exploded, but explode she did. The lodger's possessions were waiting for them outside their rooms when they arrived home. My mam told me that before grandma chucked her lodgers out she had opened their cases, inside them she found something that made her even angrier. She had left their cases open, so that they would know that she knew what was in them. Mam never disclosed what Grandma had found, just that because the D.P.s knew she knew what was in the cases, they would never come back.

Grandma eventually moved into a bungalow on a new estate but she never liked it. She said it had 'no heart', but the truth was she missed the companionship of her friends and neighbours. Her old house, she was told, had gone to a very nice family.

I didn't see John again for years, but then one time I saw him very briefly. I was at work when one morning a familiar face walked past me. It was John. He stopped for a chat then told me that he and his father had started work that very morning in the next department. I said I would pop in at break and say hello. When I got to their department later that morning they had gone. The foreman told me that when John had returned from his delivery to our department there was a heated argument with his 'father', after which his father picked up their cards and left. "I have never seen anyone leave a job as quickly," said the foreman.

Clearly they thought Grandma had shared the secret of what was in those cases.

Chapter Thirty-Two

After the long years of war and rationing the British people were slowly picking themselves up, they were beginning to rebuild their shattered country. Demobbed soldiers returned to their families with new suits and money in their pockets. But many returned as strangers to their families. Other soldiers were still missing presumed dead for these families there was no closure. The British nation was massively in debt to the American people. The bombed out factories in Germany were being fitted out with new machinery whilst we, the so- called 'Victors' had to compete with machinery we had salvaged from our bombed out factories. Everything we produced was for export, and instead of rationing ending, it had got worse with the rationing of bread.

* * *

Into this grief stricken devastated country on 22nd June 1948 the 'Windrush' sailed into Tilbury bringing young hopefuls from the Caribbean to begin a new life. Many of these immigrants had listened to the King's speech on the 3rd September 1939 and some had answered the call to arms by the 'Mother Country', and others had family who had lost their lives in the conflict. These newcomers were needed to fill the manpower shortage caused by the war which had been exacerbated by all the German POWs who had gone home, but they were not wanted by the populace. It was felt by many that the Government had been insensitive by replacing their missing and injured menfolk so quickly. The general feeling was that 'when the winter came many of the immigrants would return home to the sunshine'. But the newcomers didn't; they proved to be as resilient and hard working as the British people. They stayed, they adapted; they made new lives for themselves just as many of the ex-German POWs and D.P.s from the Soviet occupied countries had done.

But at the same time as the migrants were sailing from the Caribbean to England, British children were being shipped thousands of miles away to the Commonwealth. Some had been orphaned by the ravages of war, but many were being sent without the knowledge of their parents. One brave lady got up out of her sick bed, dashed down to Liverpool docks and rescued her twins who were already on a ship bound for Canada just minutes before it sailed. That brave lady was my grandson Alex's great grandma.

It simply didn't seem to make sense that men were coming into the country at the same time that children were being sent away.

But did we learn anything from the war? Well no, not according to Dad. He believed that one day Germany would rise again to conquer Europe with stealth and finance.

Now, almost all the factories in and around Leyland that were so crucial during the war are gone, replaced with houses and supermarkets. One of the few things left is the old Leyland Motors clock, with the attached motto: *'Leyland Motors, for all time'*, so maybe Dad was right?

Part of John of Gaunt's speech, Richard II Act II Scene I.

This Sceptred Isle

This royal throne of kings, this sceptred isle,
This earth of majesty, this seat of Mars,
This other Eden, demi-paradise,
This fortress, built by nature for herself
Against infection, and the hand of war,
This happy breed of men, this little world,
This precious stone set in the silver sea,
Which serves it in the office of a wall,
Or as a moat defensive to a house
Against the envy of less happier lands;
This blessèd plot, this earth, this realm, this England,

– William Shakespeare

TIMELINE

- 1938 – 20th August; Gracie Fields opens the Royal Ordinance Factory (R.O.F.) at a Sports and Gala in the grounds of Liseaux Hall, whittle-le-Woods in Lancashire.

- 1939 – 3rd September; Britain declares war on Germany. A law giving the Government the power to conscript men between eighteen and forty-one into the Armed forces is passed the same day.

- 1939 –Tommy Handley begins broadcasting I.T.M.A. on a regular basis.

- 1939 – 16th September; Petrol rationing was introduced.

- 1939 – 29th September; National Registration Day, the census which would be used for identity cards and rationing is carried out.

- 1939 – 21st October; Men aged twenty to twenty-three are the first batch of people required to be assessed for military service. This started the process of conscription which would see 1.5m men called up for the Armed forces by the end of the year.

- 1940 – Britain experienced a bitter winter making travel almost impossible.

- 1940 – 8th January; Food rationing introduced.

- 1940 – 10th May; Neville Chamberlain resigns as Prime Minister. Winston Churchill becomes Prime Minister and forms a Coalition Government, just as German troops enter Belgium, France and the Netherlands.

- 1940 – May; Internment for 'enemy aliens', which saw the Isle of Man nicknamed 'The Island of Barbed Wire' begins. Many were refugees from Hitler's Germany, who following an outcry were soon released..

- 1940 – 14th May; Anthony Eden calls for volunteers to join Local Defence Volunteers (Home Guard).

- 1940 – 26th May – 4th June; The evacuation of troops begins in an operation to rescue 338,226 Allied troops from the beaches of Dunkirk by a flotilla of little ships many of them tied up with ropes attached to larger vessels. Around 220,000 troops were rescued from other ports.

- 1940 – 13th June; Ringing of Church Bells was banned. They were only to be rung by the Army or Police to warn of an enemy invasion.

- 1940 – The Battle of Britain begins.

- 1940 – July; Hitler demands the surrender of Britain.

- 1940 – 11th August; Churchill signs a ninety-nine year Lend and Lease contract with America giving them the use of Britain's naval bases in the Caribbean and Bermuda in return for financial help and fifty elderly ships.

- 1940 – 20th August; Winston Churchill pays tribute to the Royal Air Force involved in the Battle of Britain.
- *'Never in the field of human conflict has so many owed so much too so few.'*

- 1940 – 14th November; Under a full moon, Coventry was bombed by 515 planes under the code name of 'Moonlight Sonata'. Around two thirds of the buildings in the city were damaged.

- 1940 – December; Probably the most devastating attack of the London Blitz, dubbed the *'Second Great Fire of London'*, with a greater area damaged than had been by the fire of 1666.

- 1941 – February; William Joyce (Lord Haw-ha) broadcast to the British nation.

- 1941 – 1st May; Liverpool was bombed for seven consecutive nights, causing significant damage to the city and the docks.

- 1941 – 4th May; Clocks go forward two hours, introducing double-double summer time.

- 1941 – 10th May; The German Deputy Fuhrer, Rudolf Hess parachutes into Scotland, trying to negotiate a policy of non-confrontation between Germany and the UK.

- 1941 – 1st June; Clothes rationing introduced.

- 1941 – 7th December; The Japanese attack Pearl Harbour inflicting grave damage to the American Fleet. Japan also attacks British territories in Singapore, Malaya and Hong Kong.

- 1941 – 8th December; Britain and America declare war on Japan.

- 1941 – 18th December; Conscription is extended with the potential to call up men and women from eighteen to sixty for some form of national service. Men from forty-one to fifty-one could now be conscripted into the military. The list of 'Reserved Occupations' which meant those in certain occupations were exempt from conscription, is abolished.

- 1942 – 26th January; American troops arrive in the United Kingdom.

- 1942 – 21st March; The 'Making of Civilian Clothing Restriction Orders' are introduced, which enforce stricter rules on clothes rations. This, and another order in 1943 cuts the number of clothing coupons for adults. Amongst the restrictions, trouser turn-ups are banned, the number of buttons and pockets are limited, and heels were limited to two inches. Also wearing a belt with braces became unlawful, you could wear one or the other.

- 1942 – 1st July; Petrol rations for civilian use are abolished.

- 1942 – 2nd December; The Beverage Report, which called for the post-war creation of the National Health Service, is published.

- 1943 – 25th April; On Easter Sunday, Church Bells are allowed to be rung again.

- 1943 – May; Conscription of women extended to single women between the ages of eighteen to forty-five.

- 1943 – 16th – 17th May; 617 Squadron (The Dam Busters) attack industrial targets in the Ruhr Valley, using the Barnes Wallis bouncing bomb which was built at Euxton.

- 1943 – 25th June; The 'Battle of Bamber Bridge'.

- 1943 – 2nd December; It is announced that from now on, one in ten men conscripted would be sent to work in the coal mines, becoming known as the 'Bevin Boys'

- 1944 - 6th June; D-Day under the code name of operation 'Overlord' allied troops land on the beaches of Normandy opening up the road to victory.

- 1944 – 3rd August; The 1944 Education Act which brought in the '11 plus' exam and raised the school leaving age to 15 became law.

- 1945 – 15th April; British Troops liberate the Belsen-Bergen Concentration Camp.

- 1945 – 8th May; VE Day as Churchill announces the end of the war in Europe.

- 1945 – 5th July; The General Election takes place. Counting was delayed for another three weeks because of the northern wakes weeks and until the overseas service personnel vote could be added, producing a landslide victory for the Labour Party. Clement Atlee becomes the new Prime Minister on 26th July.

- 1945 – 6th August; America drops an atomic bomb (Little Boy) on Hiroshima, Japan.

- 1945 – 9th August; A second atomic bomb (Fat Man) was dropped on Nagasaki, Japan.

- 1945 – 15th August; VJ Day as Japan surrenders to the Allies. W.W. 2 is now over.

- 1946 – 26th January; The first American war brides sail from Southampton on the luxury ship S.S. Argentina, carrying 452 war brides, 173 children, and 1 war groom. They receive a maritime welcome in New York.

- 1946 – 23rd February; The Queen Mary sails from Southampton to America with war brides

- 1948 – 2nd June; The WINDRUSH dock at Tilbury bringing young hopefuls from the Caribbean to England.

- 1948 – 24th June to 12th May 1949; The Berlin Air Lift.

- 1948 – December; The last of the German prisoners of war is repatriated